The Changing MO
of the CMO

The Changing MO
of the CMO

How the Convergence of Brand
and Reputation is Affecting Marketers

MARYLEE SACHS

GOWER

Published by
Gower Publishing Limited
Wey Court East
Union Road
Farnham
Surrey, GU9 7PT
England

Gower Publishing Company
Suite 420
101 Cherry Street
Burlington,
VT 05401-4405
USA

www.gowerpublishing.com

British Library Cataloguing in Publication Data
Sachs, MaryLee.
  The changing MO of the CMO : how the convergence of brand
  and reputation is affecting marketers.
  1. Marketing personnel--Attitudes. 2. Marketing--
  Management--Case studies. 3. Corporate image. 4. Public
  relations personnel--Attitudes. 5. Interprofessional
  relations.
  I. Title
  658.8'0019-dc22

Library of Congress Cataloging-in-Publication Data
Sachs, MaryLee.
  The changing MO of the CMO : how the convergence of brand and
reputation is affecting marketers / MaryLee Sachs.
     p. cm.
  Includes index.
  ISBN 978-1-4094-2315-7 (hardback) -- ISBN 978-1-4094-2316-4
(ebook) 1. Branding (Marketing) 2. Public relations. I. Title.

  HF5415.1255.S23 2011
  658.8'27--dc22

                                                    2011009092

ISBN   978-1-4094-2315-7 (hbk)
ISBN   978-1-4094-2316-4 (ebk)

Printed and bound in Great Britain by the
MPG Books Group, UK

Contents

List of Figures
and Illustrations

LIST OF FIGURES

LIST OF ILLUSTRATIONS

List of Tables

About the Author

MaryLee Sachs has over 25 years of experience in integrated marketing, most recently as US Chairman and Worldwide Director of Consumer Marketing for PR giant Hill and Knowlton. She has worked with and advised many blue chip organizations including Procter and Gamble, Kellogg's, PepsiCo, HSBC, Motorola, American Express, Frito-Lay, Porsche, Kodak and Anheuser-Busch.

MaryLee has been based in the US for the last nine years where she has been an active member of the Marketing 50 and an advisor to The CMO Club. She served as a jury member for the PR category in its inaugural year at the Cannes Lions International Festival of Creativity in 2009, and she is a member of the Marketing Group of Great Britain, the Marketing Society (UK), PRSA and Advertising Women of New York.

List of Abbreviations

AOR	Agency-of-record
B2B	Business-to-business
B2C	Business-to-consumer
BOA	British Olympic Association
BTA	British Tourist Authority
BU	Business unit
CCO	Chief communications officer
CEO	Chief executive officer
CMO	Chief marketing officer
CPRF	Council of Public Relations Firms
CRM	Customer relationship management
CSR	Corporate social responsibility
ER	External relations
GE	General Electric Company
GO	Growth officer

HR   Human resources

IBM   International Business Machines

IOC   International Olympic Committee

KPI   Key performance indicators

LOCOG   London Organising Committee of the Olympic Games and
            Paralympic Games

NGO   Non-governmental organization

OTS   Opportunities to see

P&G   Procter and Gamble

P&L   Profit-and-loss

PR   Public relations

PRSA   Public Relations Society of America

R&D   Research and development

SVP   Senior vice president

VP   Vice president

Acknowledgements

This book was a fact-finding journey which began when I was asked by the Marketing 50 where PR should reside in an organization. Of course, there is no one right answer and what started as a white paper for the Marketing 50 germinated into a broader search for an answer, or at least some guidance.

I am eternally grateful to those people who helped me find some answers, particularly those who agreed to be interviewed, who opened up their doors and let me peer into their organizations and by doing so, contributed to and curated this book. All of them are to be congratulated for their vision of integration, and for being bold enough to create a new mantra for their organizations.

- Laurence Bresh, Marketing Director, VisitBritain

- Hugh Chambers, Chief Commercial Officer, British Olympic Association

- Beth Comstock, Chief Marketing Officer and Senior Vice President, GE

- Amy Curtis-McIntyre, Senior Vice President, Marketing, Old Navy

- Roger Frizzell, Vice President, American Airlines

- Jeffrey Hayzlett, former Chief Marketing Officer, Eastman Kodak Company

- Jon Iwata, Senior Vice President, Marketing and Communications, IBM

- Danette Leighton, Chief Marketing Officer, Pac-12

- Ann Lewnes, Senior Vice President, Global Marketing, Adobe

- Harry Pforzheimer, Chief Communications Officer and Corporate Marketing Leader, Intuit

- Darryl Seibel, Head of Olympic Media and Communications Strategy, British Olympic Association

- Simon Sproule, Corporate Vice President, Global Marketing Communications, Nissan Motors

I would also like to thank colleagues who provided stimulus and philosophical conversations as I ordered my thoughts including: Julie Atherton, Hugh McGilligan, Ruth Pestana, Lori Robinson, Tony Burgess-Webb and Paul Taaffe.

And finally, I'd like to thank my husband, Malcolm Beadling, for giving me the space in what little spare time I had to research and write the book.

Introduction

Not so long ago public relations executives had to fight for a seat at the table to be heard, to plan, to play an integral role in the organization's business – the table being the board of an organization or a senior decision-making group. Now, public relations (PR) has risen in such importance that a debate has emerged over where it should sit within an organization. Chief marketing officers (CMOs) and the senior-most marketing leaders are fairly unanimous that at least part of the PR function should reside within marketing departments, and in many cases, CMOs already have laid claim to PR within their own organizations.

What has prompted the question and sparked such a healthy debate over the ownership of PR? Certainly the growth of social media and the necessary skills to navigate two-way communication have given PR an edge over more traditional "push", one-way marketing approaches. And as reputation, credibility, authenticity, and transparency have become more important to consumers, PR has emerged as a key element of the marketing mix.

But while all indicators are pointing to increased effectiveness when the two disciplines are combined, the battle continues to brew over who reports to whom and how the disciplines work together. Many PR professionals consider "PR as part of the marketing mix" as blasphemous because, in their view, PR is a much broader management discipline which should report directly to the chief executive officer (CEO) in all cases. At the same time, some marketing executives are professionally jaundiced towards PR, considering it only tactical at worst, and an imprecise practice which is too difficult to measure at best.

Many organizations are struggling with the optimum mix of disciplines to best-harness influence and advocacy, particularly with the increasingly empowered consumer made possible by social media. The shift in power for

PR is new, and only just starting to take hold within some organizations, while others are only just beginning to consider the options.

Marketers are embracing PR and agree that integrated communications increases overall effectiveness, but while marketing and PR have formalized working relationships in some cases, data suggests that "formal" doesn't necessarily mean "functional," according to a study undertaken by Vocus,[1] surveying 966 PR professionals about their perceptions of integrated communications. "Despite formalized processes or structures, 34 percent cited organizational structures, functional silos, or turf battles' as the single largest barrier to integration. The next largest barrier is budget shortcomings with 20 percent of respondents."

In many cases, structures are not even formalized though. Forbes[2] reported that advertising (92 percent), research (85 percent), and PR (73 percent) are top functions falling under the purview of marketing, followed distantly by internal communications (58 percent) and corporate social responsibility (51 percent). But according to a 2010 survey of CMOs by The CMO Club,[3] while the synchronization of brand reputation and brand image is more critical than ever, more than half (52 percent) of companies are not fully aligned between marketing and communications. CMOs who report the highest levels of alignment between marketing and PR establish objective-setting with blended and collective rewards. Firms where joint metrics and joint rewards systems have been created (66 percent) or joint objectives without joint reward systems (71 percent) report much higher levels of being "fully aligned" compared to firms where objectives are not shared (31 percent) or where objectives are shared only for information purposes.

The growth of digital and social media has contributed to a new landscape where marketers lack control over how their brands are perceived. Credibility, trust, and relevance are becoming increasingly important to consumers who view traditional marketing and advertising as irrelevant and suspect. The concept of "truthiness," a word coined by American television comedian Stephen Colbert, has underlined the importance of transparency and has popularized it within urban culture.

---

1   Delaria, K., Kane, J., Porter, J., Strong, F. April 29, 2010. *Blurring Lines, Turf Battles and Tweets: The Real Impact of Integrated Communications on Marketing and PR*. [Online] Available at: http://www.vocus.com/email/10/May/WP/IntegratedComSurvey.pdf [accessed: December 18, 2010].
2   Forbes Insights, November 2009. *The Role of the CMO: Marketing Strategies for 2010*.
3   CMO Club survey conducted online with 129 chief marketing officers in The CMO Club responding between May 25, 2010 and June 2010.

PR can step in and address credibility issues by providing authenticity and relevance due to its conversational nature as well as the element of third-party endorsement and advocacy.

PR also can provide the glue across paid, owned, and earned media channels. According to a Nielsen report on Advertising Effectiveness,[4] the key to success for marketers is creating a mix of social impressions that incorporate both paid and earned media. "Social advocacy and earned impressions can impact consumers in three important ways: by making them more likely to notice an ad (ad recall), to take away its message (awareness), and to increase their interest in making a purchase (purchase intent). The next step is to expand this understanding to offline sales and long-term brand value."

Even Forrester[5] suggests that owned and earned media become as important, if not more important, than paid (bought) media. Although there will always be a role for paid media, it does face several challenges including an increasing level of clutter, falling response rates, and less credibility than owned and earned media. "People simply don't trust paid media as much as other sources of information. More than 40 percent of US adults online agree with the statement, 'The experience I have with most products does not equal the promises made by their advertisements'."[6] It is certainly in the CMO's best interest to expand their power base and own the function that can address some of these issues.

And let's not forget the whole area of crisis management and communications. In what was hailed mid-2010 as the "year of the recall" by *Advertising Age*,[7] PR professionals have enjoyed newfound respect as able navigators of an uncontrollable environment in which negative word-of-mouth can be exponentially painful to brand health.

Undoubtedly, the myriad of aspects and issues connected to social media have provided the practice of PR with the opportunity to take a more central role in marketing, and there even appears to be a trend for senior executives with PR backgrounds to take the helm of marketing departments within organizations.[8]

4   Nielsen, 2010. *Advertising Effectiveness: Understanding the Value of Social Media Impression*. [Online: April 2010]. Available at: http://uk.nielsen.com/site/documents/SocialMediaWhitePapercomp.pdf [accessed: July 26, 2010].
5   Corcoran, S. 2009. *No Media Should Stand Alone*. [Online: December 16, 2009] Available at: http://www.forrester.com/rb/research [accessed: September 3, 2010].
6   VanBoskirk, S. 2009. *Consumer Advertising Attitudes Rebound*. [Online: July 13, 2009] Available at: http://www.forrester.com/rb/research [accessed: September 3, 2010].
7   Parekh, R. August 30, 2010. *Glut of Recalls Threaten to Desensitize Consumers*. Advertising Age. [Online] Available at: http://adage.com [accessed: December 18, 2010].
8   Bush, M. September 21, 2009. *How PR Chiefs Have Shifted Toward Center of Marketing Departments*. Advertising Age. [Online] Available at: http://adage.com [accessed: January 21, 2010].

With CMOs' roles expanding, how best can they prepare for their new responsibilities? Who should be in their "kitchen cabinet"? Where can they get the best advice? PR grounding can be the polar opposite of the other marketing disciplines where it's possible to define and dictate content and messaging, guarantee space and frequency. If PR is a less-understood and sometimes maligned discipline, how can CMOs fully utilize and leverage it?

Given this new landscape and the blurring roles, this book explores how some organizations are making the most of a blended approach through a series of interviews with CMOs who, in their own right, are change agents in their organizations. All of these CMOs have been in the communications/PR business at some point in their career so they have a different perspective on the roles and how the disciplines are best combined to greatest effect. There is a mix of size of organization, from small to very large, as well as a mix of business-to-consumer (B2C) and business-to-business (B2B) CMOs, with roughly one-third B2C, one-third B2B, and one-third in organizations that operate in both the B2C and B2B worlds.

1 Setting Context

There is no one right answer to the conundrum of where PR belongs in an organization. Much depends on the specific organization's challenges and objectives, type of business, category landscape, and geographic reach. Historical silos, culture, personalities, and budgets also play factors, or can be hindrances in affecting change in organizations.

At the very least, one can assume that the traditional role of the CMO is changing and becoming more subservient to the customer, and that in turn is affecting strategy and structure across organizations. CMOs need to be sensitive to the symbiotic relationship between the traditional control of marketing and the stimulating and feeding of conversations with the target audiences in a much less controlled landscape. Marketing can no longer control the conversation and sometimes is even banned from it. Target audiences as well need to be defined much more broadly than just consumers or customers to embrace employees, professionals, experts, communities, non-governmental organizations (NGOs), legislators, and others. The traditional "push" marketing model is no longer appropriate given the circles of influence that have emerged. Conversation and participation have become vital.

Marc Pritchard, chief marketing and brand building officer of Procter and Gamble (P&G), said in the British edition of *PRWeek*,[1] "PR focuses on building brands anywhere consumers engage with us. Stories are the most important part of the marketing mix and are what we think about first. But we will place a lot more emphasis on PR in the future, as it's one of the most authentic ways to engage with consumers."

---

1 Singleton, D., Wicks, N. 2010. *Procter and Gamble Unveils Plans To Refocus Marketing Budget On PR*. PR Week UK. [Online: July 1, 2010] Available at: http://www.prweek.com/uk/News/MostRead/1013217/Procter---Gamble-unveils-plans-refocus-marketing-budget-PR [accessed: December 18, 2010].

In June 2009, P&G announced that brand-related external relations (ER) would report into Pritchard, leaving corporate-related ER reporting into CEO Bob McDonald. Previously, all ER functions reported into the P&G CEO. This shift was part of the formation of P&G's Brand Building Organization that "speaks to the company's commitment to both integration and investment in its brands." As reported by *PRWeek*[2] in the US, "We typically find that brand PR is the top or among the top ways that we can effectively connect with consumers," according to Chris Hassall, global external relations officer.

When Pritchard addressed the Council of Public Relations Firms' annual Critical Issues Forum in late 2010, he said, "I've seen the power of PR grow as an industry, and at P&G. In the early days, PR was about managing issues behind the scenes. In the late 1990s it was more important, but still an afterthought and used mostly to announce new product launches. It was in the mid-1990s when I led our cosmetics business that I experienced the true power of PR. I saw that PR works best when it's fully integrated into the marketing mix. I saw how PR could build emotional connections between a brand and a consumer. I saw PR build relationships and convert people into becoming brand ambassadors...Today, in my role...we have pressed the 'reset' button when it comes to building brands, and PR is central to that transformation. Now, more than ever, brands and companies need authentic engagement with people, and it is PR's time to shine."

According to Lauri Kien Kotcher, CMO and senior vice president (SVP) of global brand development at Godiva, "Alignment around all brand messages is especially critical in the increasingly multi-channel environment we find ourselves in. Marketing, selling, human resources (HR), and personal communications messages are all blending. The number of touch points keeps growing with different timelines for message development, which also makes the challenge of maintaining consistency across key brand messages harder than ever."

Another driver of combining forces is the seemingly permanent squeeze on budgets, forcing marketers to reassess every practice and approach in an effort to get more for the money. Interestingly, Forbes[3] reports that marketers with $5 million or more budgets are less likely to control PR than marketers with smaller budgets (52 percent versus 73 percent), suggesting a natural occurrence of silos in larger organizations. Equally, whether a business is a B2C or B2B may affect the thinking about where PR resides.

2   Iacono, E., Gordon, R. 2010. *Editors' Choice 2010: P&G*. PR Week US. [Online, January 1, 2010] Available at: http://www.prweekus.com [accessed: December 18, 2010].

3   Forbes Insights, November 2009. *The Role of the CMO: Marketing Strategies for 2010*.

According to a Marketing 50 One° Report[4] for its members, B2B member companies of the group were far more likely than B2C members to have PR reporting into marketing. Interestingly, dual reporting and specific corporate communications departments not under marketing were exclusive to B2C respondents. In this survey, three schools of thought emerged on organizational structure:

1. Marketing – PR is about brand and messaging, reporting to CMO.

2. Split or Dual Report – Split PR function with "customer/product" aspect reporting to marketing or single PR function, dual reporting to corporate communications and to marketing.

3. Elsewhere, but Aligned – reporting to Corporate Communications, but closely aligned to marketing.

One of the greyest areas may be internal communications which has fallen traditionally under PR. The varying degrees with which the brand is affected by its employees should help to inform strategy here. For example, retailer CMOs (together with the HR function) should have some if not total control over the internal communications function, since many employees are front-of-house and the first point of contact for the brand. They are the brand ambassadors and need to be groomed and cultivated as such. But retail or not, employees should represent an incredibly rich vein of brand advocates. Unfortunately, while having employees serve as brand ambassadors is viewed as valuable and vital, only a small group of companies currently have a fully established program to engage them in that way. In The CMO Club survey,[5] 70 percent of CMOs reported that they did not have an active employee engagement program. Nearly half (46 percent) reported working on developing a program, and 17 percent were not working on a program at all, but plan to at some stage. Only 58 percent of the CMOs surveyed in the *Forbes* Insight report[6] claimed responsibility for internal communications.

Similarly, customer service and customer relations functions are in those grey areas. And corporate social responsibility (CSR), historically the domain of the corporate brand and corporate communications function, has been increasingly used to further product brand goals, often providing an emotive avenue from which to connect to consumers.

---

4   Marketing 50 One°, April 2010. *Where Should PR Reside Within the Órganization?*
5   CMO Club survey conducted online with 129 CMOs in The CMO Club responding between May 25, 2010 and June 2010.
6   Forbes Insights, November 2009. *The Role of the CMO: Marketing Strategies for 2010.*

There are caveats. Heavily regulated industries like healthcare and financial services rely on the PR function for a deeper understanding of restrictions surrounding marketing communications. Issues and crises throw everything into disarray, and a seamless link with research and development departments, operations, and other business functions is critical. Guardianship of multi-market and international brands is even more important with the advent of the global social world online. Listening, messaging, and navigating the social media environment have become even more important, since a mishap in one market can quickly affect another.

There clearly is no one-size-fits-all approach, and some organizations create and recreate structures to accommodate trading environments, current needs, and personalities. For example, when American Airlines decided to combine its advertising and PR functions into a single group under the CMO in 2003, the team believed that they would be able to capture some important synergies by combining the two, especially in how brand and corporate reputation were managed as well as addressing emerging media, sponsorships, and promotions that often fell between the two functions. During this period, the airline launched a new brand strategy and tagline – "We Know Why You Fly" – and numerous campaigns, all tightly integrated with advertising, PR, social media, and marketing. The work resulted in dozens of industry awards, including the Bronze EFFIE for advertising effectiveness, as well as significant improvement in awareness, consideration, preference, and willingness to purchase scores, even during difficult times for the airline industry.

During this period, the marketing function included: advertising/corporate communications, the AAdvantage loyalty program, the airline's website AA.com, onboard products/services, customer relationship management (CRM), reservations, customer experience and global sales/distribution, advertising sales, and in-flight products and services.

In 2010, with a new CMO coming on board, the group has been restructured and divided into two parts. The customer-facing elements of the job were moved under a new SVP in charge of customer experience, including corporate communications (including customer communications and social media), AA.com, reservations, customer experience, and in-flight services. All other remaining marketing functions moved under a chief communications officer (CCO) in marketing, underlining a growing closeness between marketing and finance. The CCO's responsibilities include: a new market planning function, advertising, and onboard products along with pricing/yield management, international planning/alliances, and fleet planning.

According to Roger Frizzell, vice president (VP) at American Airlines, "The rapid pace of technology change and the emerging social media channels continue to change how we undertake our practice. Likewise, the decline in the economy has forced the need for us all to do more with less, leveraging our resources to the fullest."

A white paper published by global executive search firm Spencer Stuart on "How high-performing CMOs exceed expectation"[7] claims that "CMOs need to be at the forefront of a host of changes impacting companies today, including advancements in technology, changing customer expectations about companies and brands, and emerging competitive threats. With the evolution of new media and social networking, companies have to figure out how to connect with consumers and allow them to be part of the brand rather than just being communicated to about the brand. They will have to master analytics to better understand customer behaviors and develop insights to inform decision making related to customer acquisition, CRM, product and service development, pricing optimization and marketing spending."

9

All of these aspects will have significant implications for marketers, and there are challenges in getting everything – and everyone – to work harmoniously together. If one agrees that marketing should own at least a part of the communications or PR piece – which include aspects like reputational intelligence, advocacy, and engagement – there's no magic formula for making it work via organization, shared goals, and/or a reward structure. But some organizations seem to have found a successful formula for working together. The next few chapters provide insights on how some CMOs have organized their marketing functions and teams to achieve their fullest potential.

---

7   Spencer Stuart, 2010. *What Do You Want From Me? How High-Performing CMOs Exceed Expectations*. [Online] Available at: http://www.spencerstuart.com/research/articles/1462. [accessed: December 18, 2010].

2 The Intuitive CMO: Intuit, Inc.

Intuit Inc., the American software company that develops financial and tax preparation software and related services for small businesses, accountants, and individuals, was founded in 1983 by Scott Cook and Tom Proulx in Mountain View, California. The company makes the personal finance programs Quicken, MINT, and TurboTax (and its Canadian counterpart, QuickTax), as well as small business accounting program QuickBooks. In addition, the company produce QuickBooks Point of Sale solution for small retailers, professional tax solutions ProSeries and Lacerte, and the web-based corporate workgroup productivity solution QuickBase.

HARRY PFORZHEIMER, CHIEF COMMUNICATIONS OFFICER AND CORPORATE MARKETING LEADER

Illustration 2.1 Harry Pforzheimer

Table 2.1   Harry Pforzheimer professional experience

2007–current:	Chief Communications Officer and Corporate Marketing Leader, Intuit, Inc.
2003–2007:	Chief Communications Officer, Intuit, Inc.
1997–2003:	President, Western Region, Chair of the Global Technology Practice and GM of technology practice hub in Silicon Valley, Edelman PR
1989–1997:	Worldwide Director of Corporate and Marketing Communications, Silicon Graphics
Prior to 1989:	Led communications for, StorageTek, United Banks of Colorado, and a subsidiary of The Standard Oil Company

Intuit seems to have been at this longer than most. The company, which was founded on the basis of inventing a replacement for paper-and-pencil based personal accounting, determined a new way for integrating its marketing and public relations functions when its CCO, Harry Pforzheimer, took on the additional mantle of corporate marketing leader. After over a dozen CMOs in its 28-year history, Pforzheimer found himself in the unenviable position of inheriting the marketing function, but with a life expectancy of just 18 months for the average Intuit CMO, he recognized the curse of the title and shunned it "just because [he] wanted to work here longer" and because the other model – that of being CCO, which always had a seat at the C-suite table – was working.

Pforzheimer then set about further restructuring the marketing department, decentralizing the function, and helping drive into place great marketing leadership in the business units (BUs), creating an operating mechanism to increase collaboration, and streamlining the organization, stripping out layers and duplication between the BUs and the center. The central marketing department of some 300 was streamlined to around 80 since much of what was done at the center was better off being done in the BUs as the businesses reach out to different types of customers.

At the center, Pforzheimer created a marketing organization committed to excellence and best practice, overall analytics and talent development (training, mobility for marketers across the company, marketing communities and special interest groups). He then worked between the central group and the marketing leadership team – the marketing leaders of the BUs – to ensure a high degree of consistency from a performance perspective, and deployment of best practices. According to Pforzheimer, it's working so much better than having a large

Communications & Central Marketing

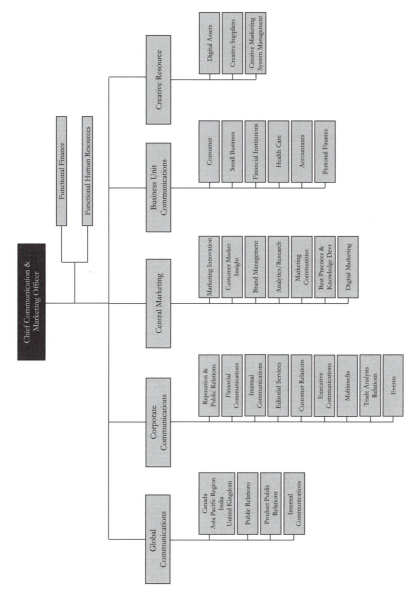

Figure 2.1   Intuit organizational chart

central organization that has perceived power but little budget because the product budgets reside in the BUs alongside the revenue responsibility.

It has proven successful. The company only started advertising in the last six years, expanding its marketing armory from direct mail, PR, events, and other marketing efforts. Advertising collectively across the BUs has reached over $100 million per year, in turn reaching an additional 3 billion customers. But in the seven years that Pforzheimer has been with Intuit, marketing impressions have increased from 1.5 billion to over 17 billion, excluding advertising. Brand visibility and product awareness historically has been driven by PR. Intuit has 55–60 million customers, and eight out of ten of those sales come via word-of-mouth. So communications is one of the few efforts or functions within the company that's completely consolidated at the center since, in Pforzheimer's view, a decentralized communications/PR function is a disaster because the only way to get a high degree of consistency and credibility is to have all of the PR operations together. The central team includes experts in business and financial media relations, product PR specialists, a multi-media group, analytics specialists, and an internal communications team.

Social media, on the other hand, is a part of everyone's job, and Intuit is establishing a solid track record in experimenting in the space. With Twitter alone, Pforzheimer's TurboTax PR team has been able to demonstrate that the company can produce revenue from Tweets from some experiments they have run during the tax season. But it's less about using it as a sales tool; it's so much more. Pforzheimer says that the organization is so consumer-centric first that social media presents just one more tool with which to engage with customers to help them with their issues, to provide solutions, and to facilitate the conversation.

Pforzheimer reports that Intuit has a special interest group on social media that exists cross-company with marketers, PR practitioners, trade industry analysts, and others totaling more than 100 members who meet monthly for two to three hours to talk about new trends and share best practice.

Seth Greenberg, VP of global media and digital marketing at Intuit, presented on Turbo Tax – one of Intuit's BUs – at the 2010 Association of National Advertisers conference. He talked of Intuit's "social revolution" and how Turbo Tax is using analytics for data-driven decisions to drive word-of-mouth. Analytics cover everything from traditional media to experiential and digital, and look at in-channel optimization, cross-channel/platform engagement measurement, predictive analytics, and testing for impact. Interesting concepts like "friendcasting" in the age of media anarchy and the social conversation funnel which Intuit has developed are illustrative of cross-disciplined thinking and a no-holds-barred approach to marketing in the new integrated ecosystem.

Pforzheimer credits some of Intuit's marketing intuition to the company's current president and CEO, Brad Smith, who before joining Intuit, led the marketing function for ADP, and worked in marketing and sales with Pepsi, 7Up, and Advo. After joining Intuit in 2003, Smith took on his current leadership role in January 2008 as the company marked its twenty-fifth anniversary.

The BU leaders of marketing, of which there currently are 13, are considered "growth officers." The growth officer (GO) "defines those who have a responsibility to grow the [Intuit] company – by connecting customers with products and services that help them achieve their dreams."

From a planning perspective, the GOs develop one- and three-year plans which are BU-specific, based on revenues, and focused on creating growth for the company and development of the marketing function. These plans get rolled up into the overall BU business plans. Meanwhile, Pforzheimer creates one- and three-year plans at the center together with some of his central team and the marketing leadership from the BUs.

According to Pforzheimer, it took four months to create the planning process, but paving the way to think three years out has proven to be invaluable in helping the marketing leaders grow their businesses and develop their own careers. The process also aids in recruiting since it helps to define the experience needed and the kind of talent for which Intuit is searching.

A by-product but important output of creating the planning process has been development of a marketing competency model that helps to define the future marketer. Pforzheimer believes this is driven by four key elements. First, the marketer has to be strategic, strong in marketing fundamentals, and have unbelievably deep customer understanding. Secondly, they need to be connected, and effective in managing messaging in different channels. That aspect used to be more specific to the communications discipline, but it now takes into account consistent delivery, multi-channel execution, and global implications. Third, the marketer needs to be digitally savvy, to be able to leverage technology to enhance product marketing and product management. And finally, the fourth marketing excellence characteristic is being scientific, understanding analytics to be able to make data-driven decisions.

The marketing competency model also has enabled better talent mobility between the BUs. According to Pforzheimer, it's much less about getting

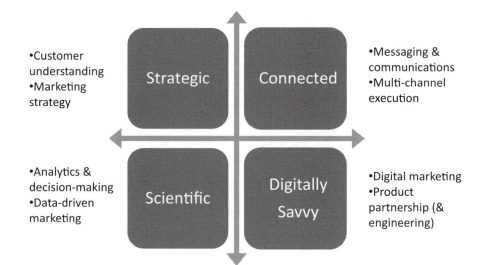

•Customer
understanding
•Marketing
strategy

•Messaging &
communications
•Multi-channel
execution

•Analytics &
decision-making
•Data-driven
marketing

•Digital marketing
•Product
partnership (&
engineering)

Figure 2.2   Intuit marketing competency model

promoted now, and more about getting a wider breadth of experience, building retention at the same time. It would appear that Intuit's employee engagement is better than most. According to an independently-managed annual employee survey with 300 questions conducted by Sirota, the central marketing communications team has ranked as the top function for engagement in the company for the past two years, globally, with a mindset calibrated to explore, do, figure out, empower and innovate.

With employee engagement at an all-time high, the combined marketing and PR team at Intuit continues to evolve. Pforzheimer believes that the lines are getting further blurred between the two areas and that there is a completely new model on its way. Overall, he says that the best people he's worked with are not just great communicators or marketers, but they understand the business. "They are just as good at strategy as they are at execution. They understand more than that. It's more than getting a message out; it's around the overall implications to a host of different audiences."

Mobility is increasing too between the marketing and PR disciplines. Training continues to be an important element of sustainable growth for this group, building and bringing in best practices, commercial innovations, and training customer benefit and BASES and A/B testing – modifying everything for the Intuit business and combining it with the leadership training that comes out of the training development team in HR.

The team continues to flourish and grow. For example, on the communications side alone, the group numbered just 15 people when

Pforzheimer joined Intuit. With "zero attrition," now it's 50, plus with the PR roster agencies, the company has approximately an additional 100 communications and PR people.

Did Pforzheimer need to learn a new marketing language when he took up the combined reins of communications and marketing? He would say yes – that even though he'd been around it, he needed to better understand it.

Meanwhile, the culture at Intuit continues to foster experimentation. Pforzheimer claims a group passion to explore with a no-fear factor and the courage to make mistakes: "I love mistakes – we're learning from them; if you're not making mistakes you're not doing anything. So there is this innate sense of exploring, learning, developing, fascination for what we do and how to most effectively communicate the message and engage in the discussion. That part has really evolved; it's not just communicating the message, it's the ongoing engagement that you now have to have."

As the model continues to evolve, so does the scope for key performance indicators (KPIs). Pforzheimer and his team take the CEO through a marketing operations review every quarter, which covers everything from number and growth of customers, stickiness (how many products they buy into across the porfolio), gains/losses in customers – and new to the franchise, total subscriptions, small business versus consumer, sales sources in terms of channel (retail, telesales, direct), marketing spend versus head count, and whether Intuit is winning in the growing online and "cloud" usage of products. According to Pforzheimer, "Most people still think of us as retail boxes and yet half of our sales and revenue is now coming from SAS (sotfware as a service) online products."

The big picture KPIs are for the CEO and business, but Pforzheimer and his team still keep tabs on the outputs and effects, especially from the communications team – launch by launch, release by release. He doesn't think anyone has really figured out the magic tool to measure PR effectiveness because it's somewhat of an art, but he acknowledges that it has become much more scientific. And here is another area where Intuit is doing quite a bit of experimentation, looking at effect in real-time, not just quarter by quarter. "We measure and research everything you can think of – and sideways, upside down – not to necessarily measure for the sake of measurement, but so we understand better how we continue to improve to enhance the measurement process, and we do it fast!"

3 The Experiential CMO: Old Navy

Old Navy is an American clothing brand as well as a chain of stores owned by Gap, Inc., with corporate operations in San Francisco and San Bruno, California. Old Navy opened its first stores in Northern California in 1994, and as of 2010, the company has 1,060 stores in the US and Canada. Old Navy's target market is price conscious though still fashion-oriented teens to adults. The clothing is more affordable than its other Gap counterparts. Old Navy stores contain specialized sections for infants, boys, girls, men, and women. In addition to clothing, Old Navy sells a variety of accessories such as shoes, handbags, toys, hats, and sunglasses, along with a line of clothing and toys for dogs.

AMY CURTIS-MCINTYRE, CHIEF MARKETING OFFICER, OLD NAVY

Illustration 3.1 Amy Curtis-McIntyre

Table 3.1   Amy Curtis-McIntyre professional experience

2010–current:	Senior Vice President, Marketing, Old Navy
2008–2010:	Senior Vice President, Marketing, Hyatt Hotels
2007–2008:	Marketing, Jimmy John's
1998–2005:	Vice President, Marketing, and founding executive, JetBlue
1996–1998:	Vice President of Marketing for North America, Virgin Atlantic Airways
1992–1996:	Director of Marketing, Celebrity Cruise Lines

Amy Curtis-McIntyre was appointed by Gap Inc. as Old Navy's chief marketer in June 2010, where she leads all aspects of marketing and brand management for the brand. At the macro level, she is responsible for developing strategies that continue the brand's momentum and drive deeper engagement with the Old Navy target customer: a young mom shopping on a budget for her family and herself. On a micro level, this includes everything from the traditional elements of marketing – which now include digital and social – to store design, windows, packaging, and new store development. She reports directly to Tom Wyatt, president of Old Navy, who joined Gap as president of GapBody in 2006.

Curtis-McIntyre is a seasoned marketer. She joined Old Navy from Hyatt, where she was responsible for developing a global brand communication strategy to differentiate and drive preference for Hyatt's brands worldwide, including the development and launch of Hyatt's first global advertising campaign and collaboration with Hyatt's HR department to communicate key brand messages internally. As the founding CMO of JetBlue, she was responsible for all aspects of sales and marketing for the successful start-up, including developing the brand platform, advertising, promotion, public relations, and web strategy. In addition, at JetBlue she managed product design and development as well as internal communication. She has lectured widely and has served as an independent consultant offering marketing and branding counsel to a variety of clients including Yahoo!, Google, Gap, Dunkin' Brands, BRGuest Restaurants and several university schools of business administration such as Yale, Kellogg, Harvard, Cornell, and Wake-Forest.

With such a varied background in marketing a number of brands, it's impossible for Curtis-McIntyre to limit her views on the changes taking place in the marketing discipline to Old Navy. But she's thankful for the marketing passion already existing in the organization: "Thankfully, delightfully, happily

Gap Incorporated is a very marketing and PR savvy organization. Old Navy took the lead from Gap, having strong marketing leadership and strong communications and PR leadership which is managed under the marketing umbrella. It was a huge marketing and PR success from the beginning."

Now a 16-year-old brand, Old Navy's marketing suffered some significant shifts at its half-life – about eight years ago – which were not helpful to the brand. "There was a foray into fast fashion, a foray into youth culture, and a foray into this, that, and the other thing," says Curtis-McIntyre. She points out that it was no mystery that until about three years ago, Old Navy was on a death watch. That's when Wyatt came to the rescue as Old Navy's new president and with his heavy retail experience, it was back to the basics that were previously Old Navy's successful formula. "He did a clean-up of spend-heavy executives; he did a clean-up of inventory; and refocused the entire organization on selling to its core target which is 25–35-year-old women," says Curtis-McIntyre.

Old Navy significantly turned around in 2009. It was a big revenue contributor for Gap, and the brand entered 2010 strong, sticking to basics. Curtis-McIntyre credits Wyatt's leadership for the turnaround but claims that Wyatt would be the first to say that he's not a marketing guy. "He understands marketing; he knows good marketing when he sees it. I think he's a really strong leader of disciplines that he's not an expert at," she says. But in all of the cleaning up, as is often the case, there was a lot of slash-and-burn in marketing. Social media was never properly developed for starters. And PR – which many didn't understand – ended up being consolidated under the senior director of media even though PR is about earned media and not paid-for media. The media director manages a $200 million-plus media budget but also has the manager of PR reporting to her, as well as a manager of publicity in New York who manages the fashion show PR. It seemed a puzzling move to Curtis-McIntyre when she arrived, but after watching the team, she believes it works well ironically.

This sort of accidental structuring came about in part due to a management exodus – some by force and some by choice, but it has worked primarily due to the personalities and collaboration involved according to Curtis-McIntyre. And one of the biggest benefits of putting paid and earned media together has been the advent of a new breed of media integration plays which traditionally wouldn't have seen the light of day given the traditional separation of church and state in the media world. With underpinnings of PR, these integrations are built around "real" stories. "If it's going to be credible, then it's got to have authentic story elements even if there was some blending of the spend," says Curtis-McIntyre.

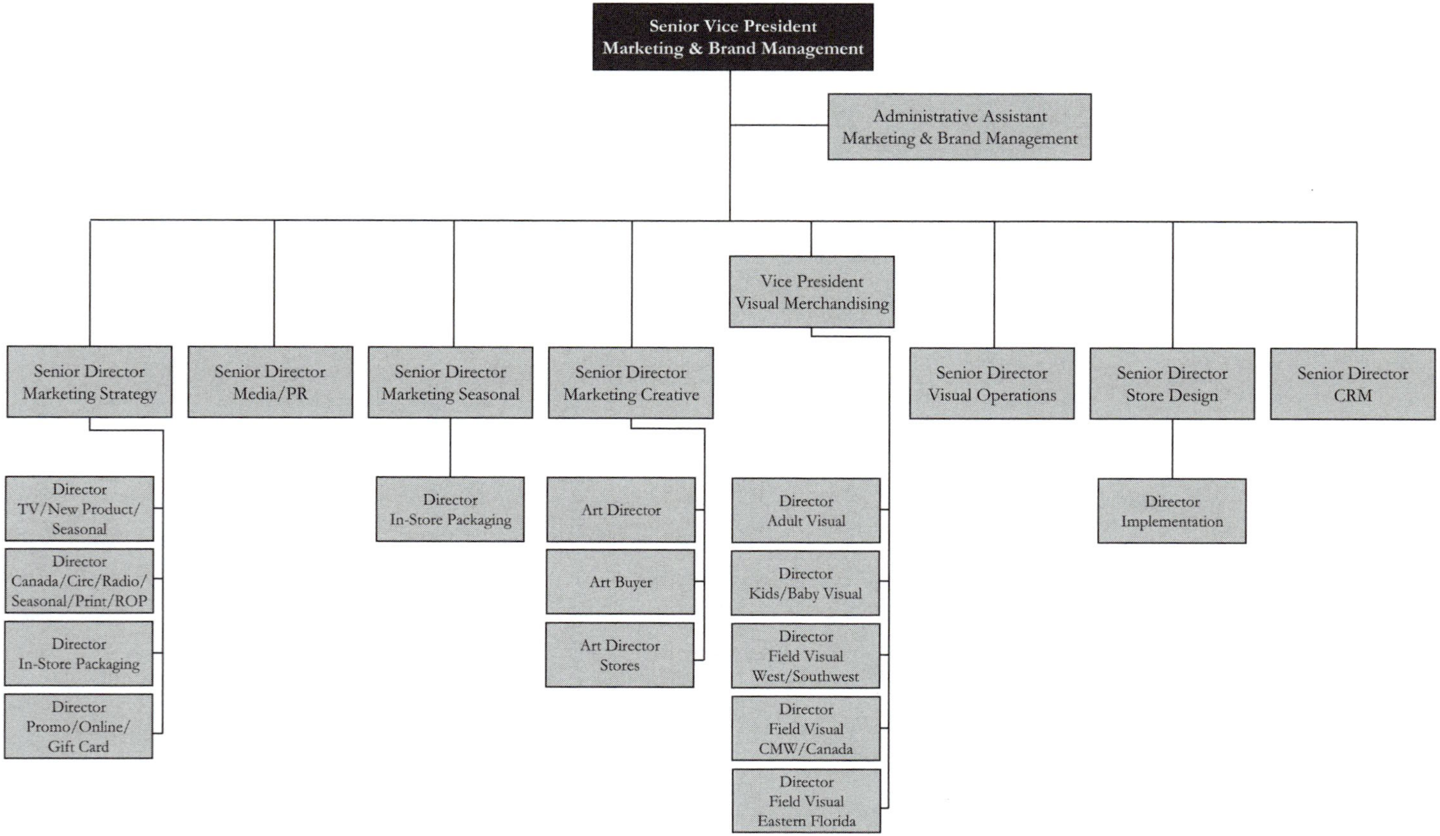

Figure 3.1 Old Navy organizational chart – directors and above

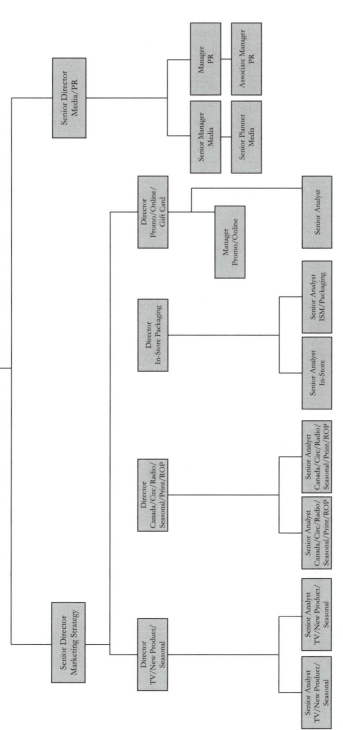

Figure 3.2   Old Navy organizational chart – strategy

Within the Old Navy organization, Curtis-McIntyre has a team of 85 including some creative folks. She has eight direct reports, each supported by his or her own team, including a number of director-level executives across the group, and PR is a critical part of her marketing strategy team.

Evaluating opportunities and holes, she recognizes that she needs to bolster her resources in digital/social media and emerging media and public relations which she currently is addressing. She also works with Gap Inc. resources. She has a corporate communications leader at Old Navy who works very closely with corporate communications at Gap, alerting them to major promotions and programs so that they are aware in terms of any potential sensitivities to corporate or financial announcements being released at the same time. Conversely, if Old Navy receives requests for business stories, these get redirected to the Gap Inc. team. Internal communications sits in three different places: Old Navy, Gap Inc. who control the intranet, and HR.

Curtis-McIntyre draws from her other marketing experiences to help guide her at Old Navy. She is aware more than most of the power of the consumer. "When you are in the travel business – hotels, restaurants, airlines, rental cars – you know that these are the products and services that people really love to celebrate or really love to shred. So Trip Advisor is your wildest opportunity and your worst nightmare, and Trip Advisor works on two levels: it's an active solicitation of marketing dollars – its business succeeds on the basis of advertising – and the reason it's so successful is because of the unbiased crowd-sourced opinions about brands or companies," she says. The beauty of the business model is that Trip Advisor has no ownership over the legitimate reviews on its site so they can't be bought off.

Curtis-McIntyre has a healthy respect for PR – she began her marketing career at communications firm Hill and Knowlton in New York where she worked with Gareth Edmondson-Jones, who coincidentally became her PR partner at both Virgin Atlantic and JetBlue. In both cases, Edmondson-Jones reported directly to the CEO, which made sense to Curtis-McIntyre because both Richard Branson and David Neeleman respectively were media rock stars, so "the more Gareth sold David, the more Gareth sold JetBlue and that was good for us all," according to Curtis-McIntyre. Despite the reporting structure, marketing and PR were joined at the hip, and all of the marketing disciplines – including advertising, digital, sales – regularly planned and ideated together around new offerings, promotions, discounted fares, new routes, and other marketing opportunities.

Curtis-McIntyre narrates a good example: "National goes out of business. JetBlue decides to go into Las Vegas as soon as possible, which turns out to be two weeks from National's demise. So Neeleman steps in and says we'll cover the Vegas service for displaced National passengers at a fraction of the current fare, and we'll start minimal service and build up. So, we have zero time to launch a new market. We get that information on a Monday and drop everything else. We get someone working on advertising with the agency, and the promotions department is thinking about what we can do on the ground in both Vegas and New York – some sort of physical guerrilla activity. We hit the email list, post it on the web and do all those kinds of things, and then we think about what kind of ridiculous noise we can make in New York. You don't need it in Vegas because it's originating there. Given that Thanksgiving is upon us, the idea ends up being an offer: the first 300 people who show up on location in New York dressed like a symbol of Thanksgiving get a free round-trip ticket to Las Vegas. We also solicited canned goods for the homeless and the posters featured the message 'Show us your cans to get in,' playing off a double-entendre of what 'show us your cans' would mean in Vegas. We put ads in the *Village Voice* and *New York Post*; we traded airline tickets for the restaurant; and we just had coffee and muffins for the folks that showed up."

It apparently was a huge success. Five hundred people turned up at 8am and JetBlue gave them all a ticket. The story was picked up by at least four NY television news stations as well as radio and newspapers, and the JetBlue Las Vegas route was on the map.

Curtis-McIntyre credits the success of programs like this to "end-to-end" thinking, blending the skills together to create maximum outcome. And she advocates for the same blended thinking and approach in tougher times such as managing through an issue or crisis when even more disciplines need to be involved including legal, HR, and finance.

The idea of blended thinking is incorporated into Curtis-McIntyre's planning process where she relies heavily on her in-house team with minimal outside agency specialists in areas like event marketing and fashion PR. Given the fast pace of retail, she doesn't run with an annual plan but instead she and her team work to quarterly plans, working a quarter and a half out at any given time. The end goal on planning is to dovetail the marketing process with product development, but given that Old Navy was without a CMO for nearly two years, Curtis-McIntyre claims to be "playing wicked catch-up" as she ramps up her team.

There had been three VPs running creative, marketing operations, and marketing strategy working to the previous CMO. Two of the three quit so the one VP of marketing strategy was left to manage everything, and not everything got done. Curtis-McIntyre is circumspect on the role of the CMO: "On a bad day, the CMO is a coordinator. On a good day, the CMO is a conductor. Connecting the disciplines is the most important thing that he or she can do." She claims that silos had emerged and the basic connections between disciplines were non-existent, so that has been her first task to address.

With regard to KPIs, Curtis-McIntyre says Old Navy has its own tools but the company also buys into industry standard measures such as the Specialty Retailer Traffic Index. Each individual campaign is measured as well in terms of volume of traffic, sales, and cost margin. And overall, brand health measures such as the emotional connection to the customer and perception in brand quality is also measured as a qualitative assessment on an annual basis.

Given that Curtis-McIntyre came from a communications background rather than being a classically-trained marketer, does she see this as an advantage? "I totally do," she says, "which doesn't mean I'm on top of my game. But at the end of the day, great marketing is great storytelling and when you start as a communicator that has to tell the story without buying the space to do so, you become better at telling that story and I think you become better at telling your client when a story isn't going to work."

Are there any disadvantages to not being a traditional marketer? "Yes, probably, but I would rather be an A-plus communicator and storyteller and surround myself with people who understand the metrics and data and can educate me. The other potential disadvantage is a better understanding of finance," says Curtis-McIntyre. "If I were to do it all over again, I would have taken more finance."

4 The Sprinter CMO: British Olympic Association

The British Olympic Association (BOA) is responsible for the UK's participation in the Olympic Games. It was formed on May 24, 1905, at the House of Commons in London. It originally had representatives of seven sports but now all 35 Olympic sports have a member. The BOA has been responsible for the UK being one of only three countries (with France and Switzerland) that have competed at all summer and winter Olympic Games since 1896. It also helped in hosting the 1908 and 1948 games, as well as the 2012 games.

Working with the Olympic Governing Bodies, the BOA selects Team GB from the best sportsmen and women who will go on to compete in the Olympic Games. It is not funded or controlled by Government, has no political interests and is completely dependent upon commercial sponsorship and fundraising income.

The BOA has a close relationship with the London Organising Committee of the Olympic Games and Paralympic Games (LOCOG) which is a limited company owned by the Government of the UK that will oversee the planning and development of the 2012 Summer Olympic and Paralympic Games. After the successful London bid, LOCOG was formed as a limited company to continue the work started by the bidding team.

HUGH CHAMBERS, CHIEF COMMERCIAL OFFICER

Hugh Chambers was headhunted to lead the commercial side of the Olympic program with the BOA after he sold out of his motorsports business in 2005. Although he has over 15 years as a sports marketer, he's always resisted the notion of becoming a sports marketing person as a self-proclaimed tag. "I think of myself as a marketer with a particular specialization in marketing

Illustration 4.1 Hugh Chambers

communications. And the reason I sort of emphasized that, I suppose, is that I think there are a lot of peculiarities in any market in which you operate. And I think they're as much a hindrance as a help," he says.

Chambers approaches the marketing challenge with a common sense approach. "You've got to start with the consumer. You've got to start with the marketplace. And I think if you ask the same, pretty simple questions in any situation, then you're going to come up with 90 percent of the answer. Where is the gap in the market? Is the market in the gap? What does the consumer want? What's really driving their motivation? How do you find a proposition which fits in their lifestyle? It's all the same whether it's marketing a rights property or a product brand," he claims.

Table 4.1   Hugh Chambers professional experience

2008–current:	Chief Commercial Officer, British Olympic Association
2005–2008:	Owner, Brand and Culture Consulting
1995–2005:	Group Sales and Marketing Director, Prodrive/BAR Honda Formula 1
1993–1995:	EVP, Marketing Practice Director, Hill and Knowlton
1985–1993:	Worldwide Client Service Director, Young and Rubicam (clients included Ford, Lincoln Mercury, Johnson and Johnson, American Express, and Monsanto)

Chambers claims that these simple building blocks probably represent a more strategic approach than other operators in the sports world. "There's a very simple reason why sports has not been traditionally commercially focused. It was focused on the sport which grew up from an amateur status and the properties were run by people who loved the sport but generally speaking they didn't have a particular marketing skills set that they brought to it. And so it's only at the point where a sport goes professional that it starts to bring in the commercial imperative, that it starts to bring in the excellence and the talent to bring in a strategic approach," says Chambers. He claims that the Olympic world has not been leading the vanguard in that respect – with exception to the International Olympic Committee (IOC).

The BOA is a privately-funded membership organization. It receives no government funding, so it has a strong commercial imperative to raise funds in order for the organization to operate and to build. And Chambers believes that the organization historically has not maximized the revenue streams from the assets and inventory it holds.

29

So the first thing he set about doing was restructuring the team around the brand and around the assets. "So what we have now is an organization which is under my responsibility which includes corporate partnerships – working with commercial partners, fundraising which represents a significant part of our revenue stream, marketing, brand, and then finally communications," according to Chambers.

One of the first things Chambers insisted on with Lord Colin Moynihan, Chairman of the BOA since 2005, was that communications should come under the marketing umbrella and not be a separate function. He believed that it needed to be strategically as well as tactically integrated. One of the main drivers was digital media. Chambers viewed a lot of the content as derived from the same sources that it would be in a PR department. The addition of user-generated content created a grey area. At the time, much confusion existed within the organization about where exactly digital fit in the marketing communications spectrum. Web management, on the other hand, was positioned within the brand management team within marketing.

He recruited Darryl Seibel as the BOA's head of Olympic media and communications strategy in early 2010. In this newly-created role for the organization, Seibel is responsible for setting strategy and developing programs to raise awareness and support for the BOA and for Team GB's athletes at home and abroad. Seibel has worked at seven Olympic Games, most recently with Team GB at the Vancouver 2010 Olympic Winter Games, and he previously was CCO for the US Olympic Committee.

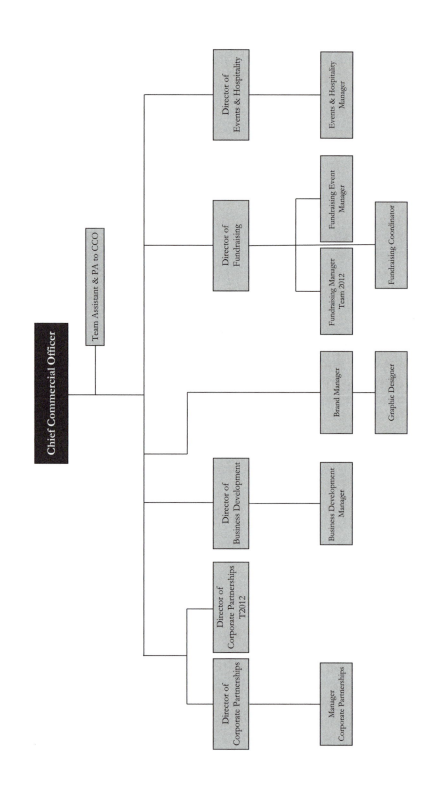

Figure 4.1   BOA commercial team 2010–2012 organizational chart

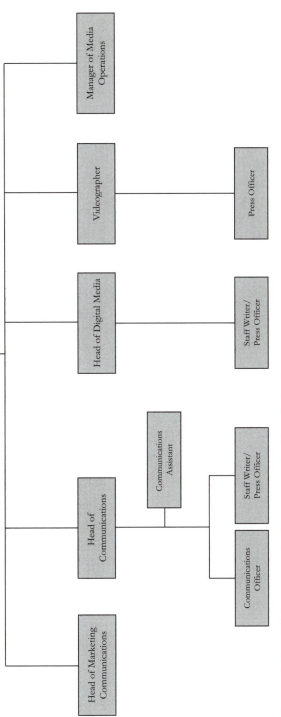

Figure 4.2 BOA communications organizational chart

According to Seibel, effective integration is less about structure than it is about access. "I think it's less important where the position resides on an org chart and more important who you actually interact with, who you have access to and, at least for an organization with a high public profile like a national Olympic committee, I think it's absolutely critical that your communications function has direct access to the CEO and the chairman of the board and other decision makers and thought leaders within the organization. Of course the comms director must be a decision-maker and a thought leader as well," according to Seibel. "So while communications is within marketing on the BOA org chart, Hugh gives me total freedom to work directly with our CEO and our chairman, and that's an understanding we've had from day one. I let him know that in order to be effective, I was less concerned about where my group sat on our org chart and more concerned about the practical nature and functional operation of the position, and he has been very supportive of that. He certainly recognizes that and we just get on with it."

Chambers continues to recruit in the build-up to the 2012 games, although he's quick to point out that the BOA won't scale nearly as significantly as LOCOG. "We only have 57 staff and we'll be building to around 120 by games time. We're split into two departments in terms of delivery to the sport: one is around performance which is led by Sir Clive Woodward, and the other is around daily operations," says Chambers. Woodward is a rock star in the UK. As head coach for the English rugby team, he led them to win the 2003 World Cup, and he will be leading a work stream around performance and technology. The operations side is responsible for selecting, managing, and transporting the team to the games, and looking after them during the games.

The LOCOG organization has already built up to 2,000 employees, and will scale to around 10,000 by Games time.

In the build-up to the Games, Chambers says that internal communications piece is more about overall stakeholder communications, "because without rattling off the list of all of the different acronyms and bodies that are involved in the Olympic space, there are dozens of them. LOCOG is just one."

To do the job, Chambers points to "a mixture of old-fashioned channels, press releases, with the latest Internet tools, conference calls, face-to-face meetings, etc." What he has found particularly useful so far are briefing sessions, and currently there are a number of these types of forums which are held on a regular basis where reports go to key stakeholders to brief them personally on status, with the opportunity for Q&A and follow-through.

In terms of KPIs, Chambers claims that the BOA historically has not had any form of tracking study or any kind of market research. "We're collaborating with LOCOG and hopefully we're going to gain the access to their tracking data which will provide us with benchmarks before we go live with our new Team GB positioning in 2011," Chambers says. The job is all-encompassing, across the board from a B2B perspective to B2C "because you need to communicate with the general population as well in terms of what's going on," according to Chambers.

The principle KPI Chambers and his team will be working to are the responses from corporate partners and the success that the organization has with renewal of those contracts in 2013, after the Olympic Games have concluded. Those negotiations will take place in 2011 and will be based around providing relevant platforms against which partners can develop their marketing programs and brand activations beyond 2012.

Additionally, the BOA will work with LOCOG on all of the licensing and merchandising programs. According to Chambers, "they have some very, very ambitious plans. In LOCOG's forecast for sales, they have about a billion Pounds Sterling of merchandising delivering a net of around 85 million Pounds of revenue to LOCOG. Around half of that is anticipated to be based upon Team GB merchandising. We obviously don't have a benchmark to measure against how we did last time. You can't just compare our performance to Beijing or Athens."

The BOA needs to build a brand on the level of scale that can deliver that sort of interest and sales. In order to facilitate that, the organization is building partnerships with people such as Stella McCartney and adidas, with whom she has worked for four years in the general consumer portfolio of products. McCartney is designing all of the Team GB competition wear in 2012, which will translate into a whole range of merchandise.

Chambers and his team are pioneering the way. He says, "the only constraint we have is we don't have any marketing budget. We're very challenged in trying to communicate to 60 million people in the UK and four billion people worldwide. The good news is that we live in a digital age and the opportunity to communicate to those audiences through digital media has been completely unforeseen anytime in sports marketing history to date."

Chambers has some aggressive and ambitious targets for how Team GB is communicated in the digital space by 2012. He's exuberant about one of the new programs launched on March 15, 2011, when, with just 500 days to go before the games, tickets went on sale and teamgb.com went online, aiming to engage the entire nation and create an effect whereby the whole country has become one team. Based on a core platform, "Our Greatest Team," and a central executional idea, "The Pledge," the program offers to inform, involve and inspire everyone by providing the opportunity for all audiences to engage, develop and mold the Olympic Games to their own needs. According to Chambers, "The campaign invites the nation to pledge their support. The objective is to create a golden thread, but to use other media channels and budgets to achieve it." His analogy is the difference between "open" and "closed source software." "We are more like Linux and Mozilla – inviting adaptation and evolution – compared to a Microsoft model of most brand campaigns."

The backbone of the program is will be provided by the Cisco Eos® Software, a hosted Software as a Service platform that enables the creation, management and support of white label community-driven websites including content targeting, asset management and site administration functionality. An added benefit is the enabling of monetization opportunities. This partnership extends Cisco's role as Official Network Infrastructure Supporter for London 2012, and Chambers believes it delivers a truly transformational development to produce the most connected Games possible.

Chambers is looking well ahead of 2012. "The challenge for the rights holders of an Olympic property is developing programs that are relevant year in and year out and not just once every four years, or maybe once every two years with the winter games. And how we translate the success in an Olympic year into programs that exemplify the Olympic movement. Social media is clearly the way in which you can develop that whole strategic thread. In other words, using the Games' time as a fulcrum to build databases, to build relationships, and engagement with consumer groups which then have life way beyond the games itself is paramount," he says. Chambers sees the opportunity in working with the organization's sponsor partners on all of the social engagement programs to ensure partner integration and to leverage those partner brands so that the relationship with the BOA becomes "symbiotic."

The additional tier is the ability to capitalize on everything that LOCOG is doing in terms of social engagement which includes all of the community, sustainability, and educational projects. At the end of the games, these programs effectively pass to the BOA and, as Chambers says, "we have to find a way of having the resources to be able to capitalize on that golden opportunity. The web and social media is clearly at the absolute heart of every single one of those programs."

According to Seibel, the BOA has gone through the traditional exercise of determining where the website sits within the marketing function. "We've studied whether the website is a marketing tool that drives on content or whether it's a communications tool that has marketing applications; is it fish or foul. And we're moving more towards it being a communications vehicle with marketing applications as opposed to being a marketing-driven vehicle that relies heavily on communications, so it will move over into my area as well as all of the digital platforms. I would tell you that we're not terribly sophisticated in this space right now, which isn't a criticism. I think many organizations are struggling with this right now, how much time do you invest in it, what are the returns and all of that. So it's moving into being more of a comms-driven platform, not just web but also social media as well," he says.

Additionally, there are the broadcasting opportunities. The BBC, who are the host broadcaster for London 2012, have made a commitment to having every single minute of competition available principally through broadband which is a complete breakthrough in Chambers' eyes. "The BBC, perhaps predictably, have named their coverage of the 2012 Games as digital coverage as opposed to broadcast coverage. I think that London 2012 is going to be historically a crucial staging point for the adoption of and the maturing of the digital space for many, many consumers worldwide," he says.

The IOC expects the percentage of access made by different target audiences to change considerably since Beijing where 31 percent of viewing was online, 15 percent of consumption was by radio, 2 percent was mobile and the rest, 74 percent, was television. For the Beijing games, there were 38 million videos stream requests versus 2.6 million in Athens. "The catalytic effect that something like the Olympic Games has on people's media consumption and their ability to experiment is enormous. I think everybody is just predicting that the digital age is going to take a big leap forward in 2012," says Chambers.

He also says that everyone's strategy around mobile is changing very rapidly. The BOA is currently reviewing a potential partnership in that space which would put the organization in "an extraordinary position" since the partner is a global leader in the digital space.

Chambers' marketing role covers primarily earned and owned media, but the organization has oversight on the paid media piece second-hand via its partners who plan to run advertising campaigns which will feature Team GB. But while it's not under BOA's budgetary control, Chambers hopes to have some strategic influence over campaigns, and both the BOA and LOCOG have right of refusal on some of the creative treatments. He says, "I think it's probably not unreasonably withheld but all of the credit has to go through LOCOG and then in some regard, we have a position on that as well."

Given Chambers' varied background, including some time in public relations, what's his view on bringing different skills to traditional marketing? He points to an evolution. "In the early 1990s, I think that in terms of hierarchy in the client's mind, the advertising agency was preeminent in terms of its strategic input. Generally speaking, the ad agency led the way in terms of creative themes and marcomms planning; and PR was one of the disciplines that was within, orbiting around advertising. Clearly that's changed a great deal in the last 15 or 16 years. I think that there obviously has been much more development of sort of a media-neutral planning. I don't think people change their spots as quickly as their words, but nonetheless, there has been a convergence."

Chambers continues by suggesting that, historically, the caliber of people who were operating in the PR space was not as good strategically as people in other disciplines or within the client organization were, and that the reason for that was because the onus for PR in the marketing mix was more tactical. And when he was in PR himself, he found it a frustrating discipline because it was very difficult to control the messaging. "At the end of the day, you can strategize in terms of where you want to take the messaging, but then ensuring that the message did actually come through was a challenge. So I think people who were successful in that era in PR were very good sales people, very good communicators with influence in the media and could make things happen. But ultimately, it's real magic and power was more of a tactical tool rather than a big overarching strategic tool."

Chambers continues, "I think that's changing and I think that the difference is digital media. There's no question that the line is fully blurred between PR and other marcomm disciplines when it comes to digital because where's the content coming from? And how much control do you have over it? How much control do you want to have over it? Because if you wanted to truly reflect your achievements and your target audiences' zeitgeist, then maybe you don't want to control it too much. You want to just allow it to flow."

One last comment from Chambers on the subject? "I think it's the most challenging environment that I ever worked in, and I can't see it getting any easier. I think it's going to get more and more complex. I think you just need to have very, very smart people working in this space who have the ability to be eminently adaptable, and continually looking for new, fresh ways of communicating."

5 The Change Agent CMO: GE

The General Electric Company, or GE, is an American multi-national conglomerate corporation operating through five segments: Energy Infrastructure, Technology Infrastructure, NBC Universal (NBCU), Capital Finance, and Consumer and Industrial. In 2010, Forbes ranked GE as the world's second largest company, based on a formula that compared the total sales, profits, assets, and market value of several multi-national companies. The company has 34,000 employees around the world.

BETH COMSTOCK, CHIEF MARKETING OFFICER AND SENIOR VICE PRESIDENT

Illustration 5.1 Beth Comstock

Table 5.1   Beth Comstock professional experience

2008–current:	Chief Marketing Officer and Senior Vice President, GE
2005–current:	President of Integrated Media, NBC Universal
2002–2005:	GE's first Chief Marketing Officer, in more than 20 years
1998–2002:	Vice President, Corporate Communications, GE
1996–1998:	Senior Vice President Corporate Communications, NBC

With an organization as large and as vast as GE, success in marketing has required the sort of rigor that Beth Comstock demonstrated when she was named GE's first CMO in more than 20 years in 2003. At that time, she helped reinvigorate marketing across the company, introducing the "ecomagination" program, Imagine Breakthrough innovations and the "imagination at work" brand campaign. In her second tenure as CMO and SVP, Comstock leads the company's organic growth and innovation initiatives, and the sales, marketing, and communications functions. She remains responsible for GE's ecomagination environmental business platform, and she has taken up the reins of the newly launched health innovation platform, "healthymagination."

In between the two CMO roles, Comstock was president of Integrated Media at NBC Universal where she oversaw the television ad sales, marketing and research teams, with a focus on new advertising innovations. She led the company's digital media development and distribution, including the formation of hulu.com, Peacock Equity, and the acquisition of ivillage.com.

Comstock "grew up in the media world" and is well-accustomed to forging new paths and exploring new territory, and she's fast on her feet. She relates back to Katie Couric and Murphy Brown when her job revolved around selling the product and using communications to drive viewership. She said that she didn't really appreciate corporate communications until she went to GE. She had been in the business for about 15 years and soon learned that investor relations played a big part in the brand. It was the height of Jack Welch's reign as CEO, so the communications job centered on investor messaging and brand building for both the company and the CEO. In her early days, Comstock also took on the responsibility for advertising, so the role was starting to morph into a more traditionally defined marketing function.

When Jeff Immelt took over the helm following Welch's retirement, the remit changed from being primarily about growth through acquisition to growth from within, around the world. Immelt's tenure as chairman and CEO started off on a low note – he took over on September 7, 2001, just four days before the terrorist attacks on the US, which killed two employees and cost GE's insurance business $600 million, as well as having a direct effect on the company's Aircraft Engine's business.

Immelt's directive was to grow through technology and get closer to the customer in all markets. He inherited 40,000 salespeople, 40,000 engineers and technologists, and very few marketers with no consistent methodologies or systems, so he also challenged Comstock to develop a more strategic marketing function which would be charged with innovation.

Comstock recognized the connection between brand building and innovation in terms of going to market as one GE brand, and set about developing a structure to deliver against the goal. She oversees the entire function which is made up of three aspects: digital, advertising, and corporate communications/media relations, which includes employee relations. At the corporate level, she is responsible for strategic marketing, enterprise sales, and two of GE's big innovation platforms: ecomagination and healthymagination.

39

In addition to the core functions, across GE Comstock has CMOs and marketing leaders at the business level, and it's a "mixed bag as to where communications sits" – sometimes communications is part of marketing, sometimes it sits separately and reports into the CEO alongside the CMO. And while these folks report directly to their BU leaders on an operational basis, they have a dotted line functionally into Comstock and her central marketing team.

Across the board, GE can boast having some 5,000 marketers and an additional 1,500 communications experts. This was a considerable change from the early 2000s. It was in 2003 when the company got serious about marketing, doubled its marketing team from 2,500 and reinstated the role of CMO at the corporate and business levels. GE created a training program to bring MBAs into the company with marketing experience, and put tools and training into place since the marketers were either being recruited from the outside or promoted from within. According to Comstock, "The ones from the outside had great marketing skills, and they were brought in to help the team and move the organization forward; the ones from within knew the company and the industry, so we had to give them marketing skills." The organization spent time on getting the people, getting them up to speed, and educating the BU about what a strategic marketing team should do for them.

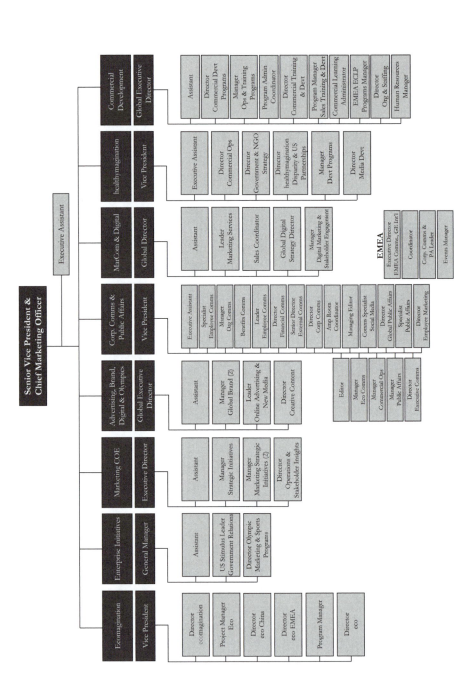

Figure 5.1   GE organizational chart

The biggest challenge with the influx of a new marketing focus and regime was the disconnect between having really great marketing talent and the businesses not knowing what to do with it.

A secondary issue was integration. Comstock started to realize as they built out the function that marketers have different behaviors, and some of them were welcomed and others weren't. "We talk a lot about marketers being instigators to drive change and fight for a better way. We found that marketers who were better at instigating didn't last as long as the ones who were really good at pulling things together," said Comstock. "To get collaboration, they generally tended to come from within the company because they knew the company, they knew how to get things done and they tended to be a bit more successful. However the instigators by and large are more innovative. The ones we called the implementers were definitely able to get more done, but perhaps didn't provide as big an innovation brain as we needed."

"It's a balance we are going through," claims Comstock. GE does a functional review three or four times a year. "The company is very big on leadership development, so we have a lot of discussion about how people are doing," says Comstock. That leads to the question of mobility – are marketers encouraged to move around the organization? Comstock says, "It's a big debate that I have with our business leaders, because I think a good marketer can go anywhere. I think you want someone with fresh eyes and perspectives to come in and see trends, even though I get a lot of push-back from our business leaders who want somebody so deep in the industries. It's a fine balance and I'd say that we don't move people around as much as I would like because of that. There tends to be some marketers who are just good chameleons – they are in different places and they do tend to move around a lot."

In any case, talent is reviewed on a regular basis and tracked. Comstock claims that GE still suffers a certain lack of innovators and instigators even though everyone can get the job done through collaboration and project management. And mobility is encouraged where it's possible and sensible. For example, GE traditionally put marketers – even product marketers – into employee communications because the internal pieces are often campaignable. And there is probably more movement between marketing and sales than there is between marketing and communications.

In 2009, Comstock and her team created a new marketing framework for the entire company along three dimensions: principles, people, and process. Within principles, GE organized eight disciplines into two groups: go-to-market activities (such as segmentation), and commercial essentials (such as

Figure 5.2   GE maturity evaluation

branding and communications). This new marketing engine was called the Maturity Evaluation and is based on "gold standard skills" and determines how GE now measures effectiveness in marketing.

Now, Comstock works across the entire group in this framework that provides opportunities to develop tools, enhance and leverage skills, and focus specifically on key initiatives such as digital. In fact, digital is such an important aspect that a corporate center of excellence has been created which consults with and supports all of GE's BUs. In terms of CMOs and CCOs, Comstock runs a Marketing and Communications Council with about 25 key people who make up this group.

Getting together is a challenge with such a large group around the world, but Comstock has used planning as a mechanism for alignment. When GE retooled its strategic planning process, Comstock and her senior marketing team played a leading role. As such, the marketing function now has a process which intersects with business planning to create a "growth playbook." This playbook is basically the marketing strategic plan, and because it's also operational with numbers behind it for the next three years, it has the adaptability to stretch as far out as a decade for long-term planning.

Comstock claims that it has taken eight years to get to the point of a well-oiled planning process, but she admits that it has been well worth the effort "to get everyone literally on the same platform."

This "rhythm," as Comstock describes it, is replicated by GE's agencies. Although the company's agency-of-record (AOR), BBDO, has been with GE for 80 years, it is now working with the new methodology. Similarly, GE's other agencies in digital and PR work with their counterparts within GE along the same organizing principle, and all of the agencies work together with plans and budgets rolled up as one. "Across the company and around the region, it's all been consolidated, so everybody's starting from the same plan and then budgeting their way forward," according to Comstock.

With regard to KPIs, the key metric for marketing is top-line growth. For a long time, until the downturn of 2008, Immelt established business targets of 8 percent to double-digit year-over-year growth, and he has held the marketing function as solely or at least largely responsible for driving new sales. The value–price equation is considered central to marketing, and although there is less of a direct sales expectation from communications, GE has the measures in place to know whether a campaign is effective. "We track all of the traditional measures in terms of impressions, click-throughs and such. There is an expectation that our efforts help bolster the sales, but I don't think there has ever been an expectation that there has to be a direct correlation," says Comstock.

Brand values at a corporate level, "big GE," and from an industry perspective are equally important across both marketing and communications, and are addressed globally by the company's Insights Group which also report into Comstock. And as greater emphasis is placed on insights and analytics, Comstock continues to build that group out, hiring a chief economist and elevating the group in terms of its importance overall. This will increase in importance as GE focus on growth markets like India, China, Middle East, Africa, Brazil, Australia, and Canada.

One of the most intriguing aspects of Comstock's job is opening new markets through innovation. "We call it commercial innovation," says Comstock, "and that means finding a new way to get to market, a new way to combine existing products into something new, and so innovation in a commercial sense is very much a goal of marketing."

Most of the GE BUs have set up a marketing leg growth board with representation from each of the business/operational functions, and there is a process for teeing up ideas, vetting them, building business plans around them, and finally funding them in a multi-functional way. Comstock calls this a "sort of green light and stage gate approach."

"We've worked really hard to make sure that technology and marketing have equal seats at the table, in terms of product innovation…" according to Comstock, "It's engineering's job to make the product, and it's marketing's job to be the GPS, the navigator, to say where it's going."

Comstock claims that GE has a wholly-defined process for this called "imagination breakthroughs," which is a pipeline of incubator businesses that are marketing-led, some with technology and some without. Immelt reviews the pipeline every month, and sometimes dives deep into the project to make sure that technology and marketing are aligned.

Of course, the two big platforms for GE are cross-company: ecomagination and healthymagination, which are Comstock's best examples of integrated marketing and communications. "Some people mistakenly think that these are nice brand advertising platforms. They are, but they also are ways we develop new customer segments and new market opportunities. We invest in R&D. We have been able to because we're looking at a specific problem we're trying to solve. It's less about functional role and more about how we solve the problem and then what marketing and communications do in support. I think when you are more externally focused, more than market focused, it's a lot easier to integrate marketing and communications," says Comstock.

Each platform serves as a kind of roadmap, a business plan and part of its success is getting the businesses engaged, centrally behind brand and revenue targets, that is, selling x-many products in its category. Additionally, there are new market development targets at two levels – corporate and business.

A practical example is GE's success in partnering with and selling to government. Ecomagination is a good tool for that since governments want clean water and better, renenewable energy, so GE can go in and create the opportunity, develop a pipeline, and work with its relevant BU to deliver against the promise. The platform allows a dialogue to be created and an opportunity to be identified; marketing opens the deal and the sales team closes it.

GE marketing works closely with sales in some cases, but it varies by business. In fact, GE has a corporate sales team that's integrated so Comstock also overseas corporate sales marketing and communications. "At the corporate level, it tends to be very much enterprise selling," says Comstock.

Specific to sales, GE has one operating mechanism called the Commercial Council. Jeff Immelt chairs it and Comstock runs it for him. The group meets every quarter and delivers reports out within the company in the intervening months between meetings. The group follows a commercial agenda for the company and sets out goals in terms of customer metrics, the contributions of the eco and healthyimagination platforms, how GE will communicate its key messages, key products and campaigns. The group which is about 30-strong from across the different businesses is fully aligned around a core set of KPIs.

The only communications function that doesn't report into Comstock is investor relations – it reports into finance, but the central teams are co-located so they operate well together.

With so much already on her plate, Comstock still is looking to grow certain aspects of the function, and identifies market research, market insights, and digital/social media as being the next spaces to develop further. "We've invested a lot in market research and market insights, but not enough to be successful. So we're continuing to grow that, understanding that sometimes the team that got you to one level isn't necessarily the team that's going to get you to the next level. Digital social media would be across all areas, but for sure communications and for sure marketing, and they are very different roles. I really do think social media is changing the landscape, and I would say our communications people probably are the most savvy ones on social media in the company because it's what they do – they connect with stakeholders, they know where the buzz is." That said, Comstock maintains that while PR has to be good at digital, marketing also has to be good at digital. "They both don't get a pass."

How are things shifting? Comstock says, "We actually are spending more than we ever have and I think we were in the depths of the economic crisis, when GE was having a tough run in financial services, and our stock was challenged a few points. And we were sick of being together in the war room mentality. So we developed an amplification strategy. It's been a great motivator for us to pull marketing and communications together because you're looking for good stories, how we tell them in different ways, and what digital does. Once we had the machine rolling, we got more funding."

Coming more from a traditional communications background, how did Comstock adapt to a broader marketing role? "I haven't come to this job with my MBA marketer's degree; I've had to learn that, so I've had a lot of real-time learning. I think there were times I felt that there was a gap, but I think in terms of experience, I've made up for it. I missed the network that more classically trained marketers bring with to their work – they have an internal and external network that I think is valuable. But I think our company has gotten instead a fresh set of eyes and a unique understanding of how media works, especially new media and technology."

6 The Traveling CMO: VisitBritain

VisitBritain is the name used by the British Tourist Authority (BTA), the tourist board of Great Britain incorporated under the Development of Tourism Act 1969. VisitBritain was created in April 2003 to market Britain to the rest of the world, and to promote and develop the visitor economy of England. It was formed out of a merger between the BTA and the English Tourism Council, and is a non-departmental public body responsible to the Department for Culture, Media and Sport. In 2005, it was voted the world's leading Tourist and Convention Bureau in the World Travel Awards. In the Webby Awards, it has been an Official Honoree in the 10th and 12th Webby Awards in the Tourism Category, and in 2008 it also was awarded the Travelmole Best Tourist Board Website award.

LAURENCE BRESH, MARKETING DIRECTOR, VISITBRITAIN

Laurence Bresh has risen through the ranks of British journalism with newspapers and latterly television, to corporate communications roles and marketing roles, and into what he now describes as a fully integrated

Table 6.1   Laurence Bresh professional experience

2009–current:	Marketing Director, VisitBritain
2008–2009:	Regional Director, Europe, VisitBritain
2003–2008:	General Manager of England Marketing, VisitBritain
Previously:	Senior communications and marketing roles including: BTA, food retailer Safeway Stores plc, e-learning agency Epic Group plc, and before taking on marketing roles, Bresh worked as a journalist for London Weekend Television and several national newspapers

Illustration 6.1 Laurence Bresh

and seamless marketing communications model. He is responsible for
global consumer and B2B marketing including the award-winning suite
of VisitBritain websites. A key part of his role will be to maximize the
opportunities presented by the Olympic and Paralympic Games in 2012.

Bresh claims that the integration – putting the consumer PR with the
marketing functions – was resisted for some time in the organization.
"Although the two teams worked very, very closely together, it was never
ultimately under one director...so we have taken the opportunity at this time,
really in the last 18 months just before I actually took up the role, to put
consumer PR in with marketing as well. So it's much more integrated now."

What was the driving force? Bresh chalks it down to the organization's move
into a new building featuring open plan on one floor so that communications
between the two functions flowed much better than when the groups
were on two separate floors. He also says that the integration was partly
forced by strategy and partly forced by budget. Over the previous two years,
the organization had slimmed down from eight directors to four, so each
director's remit had gotten much larger.

Given that Bresh had come from a PR background, he was particularly keen
that the marketing function be as seamless as possible, and he credits Sandie
Dawe, the organization's chief executive, for having the foresight to agree to
the reorganization. Dawe comes from a marketing background herself. Having
joined VisitBritain in 1991, she led marketing, business development and

publicity strategies to grow the value of tourism to Britain, and she became the organization's director of strategy and communications in 1996 before taking over the helm as chief executive in 2009.

A director of strategy still looks after the corporate side of communications, so there is still a split between functions, but Bresh maintains that it's more important to integrate fully in marketing – both in terms of marketing to consumers/travelers as well as travel partners such as travel operators – and that the corporate communications function sits well on its own to represent the organization, announce research statistics, or lobby on behalf of the industry. As well, internal communications reports up to the HR function which Bresh claims works well.

In Bresh's last year – which would cover 2010 – his role evolved. "When we talked about digital previously, we were literally talking about our websites and our CRM program. That's now evolved into social media and mobile platforms, rather than just trying to drive people to our websites. We are now syndicating our content onto third-party sites as well," according to Bresh.

A relatively new focus for TravelBritain is reaching visitors much earlier in the communications cycle. By the time people visit a tourist board website, they're pretty much on the plane says Bresh. Travelers are looking for more information and inspiration at that point, so it's to better engage during the key decision-making period, TravelBritain now works more fully with third parties such as Yahoo!, Google, and other portals, and travel partners like British Airways to reach consumers earlier in the process. Business tourism also is an important target and the organization's partner marketing team expands the reach through non-tourism partners such as film studios, the English Premier Football League – which is "a huge brand overseas," retailers such as Ben Sherman, and others.

This centralization of some aspects of the tourism marketing has served TravelBritain well in a financially squeezed environment. Five years ago, the organization had about 300 pieces of print in many different languages requiring a warehouse twice the size of Wembley – the largest stadium in Britain – to store it all. The organization has moved to two pieces of print, and Visitbritain.com has become a key tool, along with a multi-channel outreach strategy which capitalizes on social media and the integration of PR.

Bresh claims that the business has turned 180 degrees because "instead of having lots of different fragmented campaigns in 35 markets around the world, our budget just won't allow us to do that. So we're taking a much more global approach in a sense that we have now stripped down to five central campaign themes that are promoted consistently around the world. There's a much more proactive lead from the central marketing team based in London."

The five creative themes which VisitBritain now use around the world are:

- Classic Britain – the iconic aspect of Britain.

- Dynamic Britain – the more contemporary view of Britain, particular to a younger audience, which encapsulates fashion, music, film, and food.

- Luxury Britain – especially aimed at Brazil, Russia, India, and China (BRIC) markets and the emerging middle class.

- Gay/Lesbian Britain – a niche theme targeted primarily to North Americans and Australians.

- Generation Y (or even younger) Britain – which is a social media-led theme aimed especially at young Americans.

Cost constraints also have curbed TravelBritain's advertising expenditures. Bresh acknowledges that the organization cannot afford big above-the-line campaigns, so PR has become even more important. The organization has shifted funds from advertising to PR, and PR is often the lead channel. A particular emphasis is placed on getting earned media coverage in broadcast channels through the team members placed around the world which Bresh refers to as his crown jewels. "Together, they generate over half a billion Pounds Sterling worth of coverage, and over three billion opportunities to see (OTS), which is a new measure for us," according to Bresh. Of the 35 markets with TravelBritain presence, all have at least one PR operative; often but not all have marketing people. According to Bresh, in-market teams run the gamut from 10–12 people in the US, to one person in a country in the Far East, so the function cannot help but be integrated.

Another recipient of shifting spend is social media. Previously, team members were dabbling in various channels until the organization took the decision in late 2009 to get serious. Key developments included the consolidation of TravelBritain's Facebook presence into a "love UK" page which has grown organically and exponentially. TravelBritain has been rated as five out of five by Facebook in terms of its engagement. Bresh is quick to point out that a lot of commercial brands rank two or three out of five, and he admits that TravelBritain is the only destination used as a case study by Facebook. The organization also has been rated by *The Times* in the UK as last year's best national tourist office Twitter Feed. Bresh is quick to add that TravelBritain benchmarks itself against all of its key competition to analyze frequency of engagement and retweets.

Flickr has been a particular success. In early 2010, VisitBritain finalized the rebuild of its website which was reconstructed from the ground up. And whereas previously the organization would have spent tens of thousands of Pounds shooting new imagery for the site, 95 percent of the imagery came from Flickr, from real fans and travelers. The move saved TravelBritain "a fortune" and the people whose photos were featured have become advocates on Britain's behalf. Now the organization has a Britain fan base on Flickr.

On YouTube there is visitbritain.tv which has become bigger than any of Britain's individual country websites, getting a half-million views per month and housing about 1,000 videos, which are not TravelBritain videos but rather the whole UK industry videos – a great repurposing and content consolidation exercise.

To achieve everything that Bresh has done in his first 18 months, he credits the different disciplines being joined at the hip and the collaboration of his global team on strategy and delivery. They only meet together once a year in person, but it's clear that everyone is working towards a common goal. Size may help focus. TravelBritain employs approximately 350 people around the world, with about 130 based in London. Recently, with new guidelines in place, everyone has been encouraged to advocate for Britain as a destination by engaging in social media. Bresh explains that the barriers between people's private lives and their working lives are blurring, and that the organization is spreading around the world to inform would-be travelers what Britain is doing.

As the organization's success at social media builds, Bresh is backing off paid search. He still engages in search engine optimization, but he has stopped pay-per-click through the likes of Google Adwords apart from VisitBritain commercial operations where the organization is selling product. In terms of driving people to its websites, the organization completely relies on organic search, and the new website has meant that everything can be completely optimized. The numbers are still going up; proof positive that the strategy is working.

How does Bresh encourage creativity with what seems like such a well-oiled machine? He believes it's important to take people out of their environment occasionally to brainstorm ideas. He likes to kick things around and encourages his team not to necessarily look at other tourism boards, but rather examine what the commercial sector is doing, keep their ears to the ground, and to "walk the talk" by actually getting involved in social media, tweeting, and getting on Facebook.

An even newer channel for the organization is mobile, which has become a big push both in terms of inspiring people before they come to Britain, but also to provide information to them once they arrive in the UK and are traveling around the British Isles. Bresh reports the launch of iPhone apps, Google apps, and the organization is talking with a couple of mobile phone suppliers about pre-loading Britain content on to cellphones. He points to the stats that claim that by 2013, more people will be accessing the web from their mobile devices rather than PCs.

Bresh is reinventing the KPIs for the organization as well. The new fluency in social media has spawned a whole set of new metrics for engagement. The growth of PR as a key discipline has afforded the opportunity to be more quantifiable. And the business – the most important KPI – is audited by the National Tourist Office, and figures can be extrapolated to show numbers visiting, how much money has been spent, and where visitors go once inside the country.

KPIs will only become more important as the London Olympics loom closer. Bresh likens VisitBritain as the broker between UK industry and the overseas business with whom the organization works. Politically, VisitBritain has stakeholders – the Government – who want to understand what the organization does and how it can add value. The public is watching this latter aspect as well. "There is an emphasis on becoming more efficient and not wasting money," according to Bresh.

Did Bresh need to learn a new marketing language when he took up the combined reins of communications and marketing? Not really because he had been in blended roles previously, and he says that the best advice is to just roll up your sleeves and do it. He claims he's been lucky by having some great mentors who have taken him under their wing, but he hasn't been on any sort of formal marketing course except very specific skills courses in web marketing and social media.

Bresh also readily admits that he is somewhat of a technology geek – he loves digital and he loves his iPhone, so part of his success is just good timing with the advent of creativity and technology coming together. He claims that anyone who learned marketing even just ten years ago has to work hard to be completely up to date. His keen curiosity to continue learning is enormously

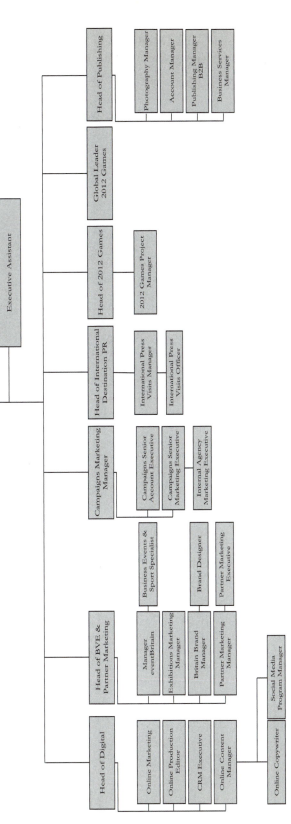

Figure 6.1   VisitBritain marketing organizational chart

The organizational chart shows the following hierarchy:

Britain Marketing Director
- Executive Assistant

Reporting to the Britain Marketing Director:

Head of Digital
- Online Marketing
- Online Production Editor
- CRM Executive
- Online Content Manager
  - Online Copywriter
  - Social Media Program Manager

Head of BVE & Partner Marketing
- Manager eventBritain
  - Business Events & Sport Specialist
- Exhibitions Marketing Manager
- Britain Brand Manager
  - Brand Designer
- Partner Marketing Manager
  - Partner Marketing Executive

Campaigns Marketing Manager
- Campaigns Senior Account Executive
- Campaigns Senior Marketing Executive
- Internal Agency Marketing Executive

Head of International Destination PR
- International Press Visits Manager
- International Press Visits Officer

Head of 2012 Games
- 2012 Games Project Manager

Global Leader 2012 Games

Head of Publishing
- Photography Manager
- Account Manager
- Publishing Manager B2B
- Business Services Manager

helpful because it's important to know what the next opportunity is, be it FourSquare, augmented reality, or other niche social technologies – all of which could provide solutions to the tourism industry.

The trifecta for Bresh is his degree in psychology – his innate interest in people and their behavior. Bresh also levels the playing field by emphasizing the importance of storytelling – no matter what the title is – which is only going to become more important in the democratized media environment.

7 The Larger-than-Life CMO: Eastman Kodak

Eastman Kodak Company is a multi-national US corporation which produces imaging and photographic materials and equipment. Long known for its wide range of photographic film products, Kodak is refocusing on two major markets: digital photography and digital printing. The company was founded in 1892 and is headquartered in Rochester, New York.

JEFFREY HAYZLETT, CHIEF MARKETING OFFICER, EASTMAN KODAK COMPANY

Named by *Forbes Magazine* as the "Celebrity CMO" for his numerous television and public appearances, Jeffrey Hayzlett was responsible for

Illustration 7.1 Jeffrey Hayzlett

Table 7.1   Jeffrey Hayzlett professional experience

2006–2010:	Chief Marketing Officer and Vice President, Eastman Kodak Company
1985–2006:	Public Relations and Communications, Hayzlett and Associates

the company's worldwide marketing operations, including the design and implementation of all marketing strategies, investments, policies, and processes. He led the company's efforts for strategy and planning, marketing programs, marketing network operation, brand development and management, business development, and corporate sponsorships. He also oversaw Kodak's corporate communications, public relations, and public affairs organizations.

Drew Neisser, CEO of Renegade and *Fast Company*[1] correspondent, interviewed Hayzlett shortly after he left Kodak and determined: "This is not your typical marketing maven. Jeff Hayzlett actually puts the chief in CMO. Instead of talking about ad campaigns, we talked about products and value propositions. Instead of talking ideas, we discussed what a marketing chief needs to do to succeed in a rapidly changing media landscape. It's not that Jeff doesn't care about ideas, it's just that he knows those are by products of performing the CMO job as a true leader."

One of the first things Hayzlett tackled when he became CMO was negotiating the consolidation of PR disciplines which were split between PR reporting to marketing and corporate communications reporting to legal. While he kept the PR and public affairs function separate from marketing, it all reported into him centrally. Internal communications remained split between marketing and HR, so aspects that were more HR-related came from that department and marketing would work with HR on announcements and internal management of the intranet. He had B2B marketing, B2C marketing, marketing operations, design strategy, and corporate communications and public affairs. Social media was included in the branding and advertising group under the "convergence media" nomenclature.

Hayzlett operated a matrix structure. Of the global marketing team, roughly 11 percent of the full team of around 800 reported directly to him. The remaining marketers reported to their BU heads. He believes in a very thin layer at the corporate level, with the majority of the marketing people

---

1   Neisser, D. 2010. *How Kodak's Jeff Hayzlett Put the Chief in Chief Marketing Officer.* [Online: May 24, 2010] Available at: http://www.fastcompany.com/1651630/how-jeff-hayzlett-put-the-chief-in-cmo [accessed: December 18, 2010].

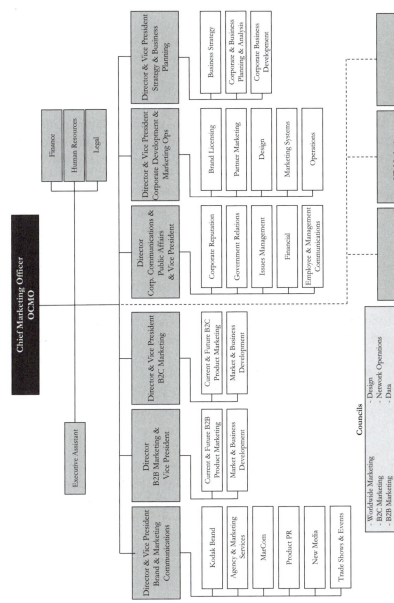

Figure 7.1   Kodak office of the chief marketing officer organization

embedded in the businesses. "That's a very philosophical thing that I have always believed in. Take out as much overhead as you possibly can." But whether solid or dotted line reporting, all of the marketing people reported to Hayzlett in one way or another, and he had governance over all of the marketing dollars spent in the businesses.

One of the other things Hayzlett did upon taking up the marketing reins was to try to instill a culture of risk-taking: "I told everyone that no one's gonna die. If you make a mistake, it's okay in the spirit of innovation." He likes tension and he encouraged experimentation backed up by measurement and learning. When speaking at the Public Relations Society of America (PRSA) International Conference in October 2010, he even referenced that his job as CMO was to cause tension: "I was the chief tension officer. My job was to take everybody to the center of the table and move them to the edge of the table."

The annual business planning was driven by the BUs but laddered up to Hayzlett so that targets, objectives, budgets, and other aspects were coordinated alongside new product launches. Hayzlett formed a number of councils in the marketing groups across the businesses that would meet on a periodic basis to drive the business forward. At that time, when new products were released, it was more like they "escaped," and this term has been used by many technology companies to characterize their product launches. Hayzlett agrees, "I said that it used to be that the products really didn't get released. They escaped. They basically found ways to be able to break loose."

As a result, Hayzlett changed the way Kodak went to market with new products. Kodak has roughly 20 product groups, each with an average of ten different product categories. That equates to 200 product categories across the company, and there would be two updates per year to each. That's 400 updates – or over one product release per day. "No organization can accommodate that sort of release schedule because it means that every day a sales person needs to be trained and updated on more than one product a day, including weekends, so that's ridiculous. So what we did was create a windows process, a planning process that we put in a marketing network architecture that would allow us to do proper planning and release products at least twice a year. We called it 'spring windows planning' for going to market in the fall, and 'fall windows planning' for going to market in the spring."

Hayzlett likens this to putting a stake in the ground based on the nature of the business. And he created an agency council with his key agency partners to work alongside the marketing councils in the windows planning process. Most of the planning was done centrally with "everything going back to the mother ship," but the organization started branching out and some of its council meetings were held off-site, including within markets in Europe. And in addition to central planning, regional planning meetings were held in all regions.

The result of the new planning process was that while product launches were not always globally simultaneous, when they weren't, they typically occurred within a month or two of the original release in the primary country of origin.

KPIs for the marketing function were primarily across three main areas: growth in sales, growth in margin, and increased satisfaction. More specific metrics existed around specific products and services, but overall, all the marketing activity was aimed at driving more sales, more profit, and to ensure that the customers were happy with the product.

Kodak's businesses were also grouped into three categories to determine the level of marketing investment they warranted: cash generators, growth products, and transformation products or businesses. Cash generation businesses received limited marketing support – enough to sustain the cash generation that the business was providing. Growth businesses typically received much more investment including the majority of advertising dollars, marketing support, and attention. Investment in transformation businesses was based on the service, the intensity of activity in the category and/or expected return.

While developing a standard marketing architecture and planning process across the company, Hayzlett also recognized new skills sets required including building out a more robust social media/digital marketing discipline. In early 2010, he hired a chief listening officer "to bring scale" to all of Kodak's social media activities, and he contracted services such as PeopleBrowser viral analytics, and had he stayed on at Kodak, his next level of work would have been increasing Kodak's use of online focus group research and qualitative online studies through organizations such as Itracks.

Market research and data management did not report into Hayzlett's marketing organization although governance of the group was in conjunction with marketing. As well, customer service reported into operations. But Hayzlett is quick to point out that, "Just because it sits outside doesn't mean we don't have a say in what's happening. If you're a good, innovative and growth-oriented company, you don't necessarily get territorial about where functions sat but more about how to get things done."

Given that Hayzlett came from a communications and business background, did he find that helpful? "Yes, I think I focus more on the results sometimes and less on the how. Even though the how is important, it was always about driving results. So I wasn't too concerned about how we got there; it was just that we got there," he replies. Were there any disadvantages? Hayzlett seemed to surround himself with other smart people so he claims that he always had someone with the right expertise to be able to help. "As long as you have a management style and allowed that to happen, then you're okay," he said.

Since leaving Kodak in May 2010, Hayzlett has poured his creativity and entrepreneurial skills into play, launching ventures that blend his leadership perspectives, insights into professional development, mass marketing expertise, and affinity for social media. He is a well-traveled public speaker and the author of bestselling book, *The Mirror Test: Is Your Business Really Breathing?*

Hayzlett also continues to contribute to the marketing profession. He currently sits on the Business Marketing Association board of directors and is a past chairman of the BMA. He's a member of the advisory board of the CMO Council, chairman of the Sales and Marketing Executives International (SMEI) Foundation for Marketing Education, a permanent trustee of the SMEI Academy of Achievement Sales and Marketing Hall of Fame, and a two-term past chairman of SMEI.

8 The Player CMO: The Pac-12

Formally the Pacific-10 Conference until January 2011, the Pac-12 is a college athletic conference which operates in the western United States. It participates in the NCAA's Division I; its football teams compete in the Football Bowl Subdivision (FBS; formerly Division I-A), the higher of two levels of NCAA Division I football competition. The Conference's members are primarily flagship research universities in their respective regions, well-regarded academically, and with relatively large student enrollment, and they compete in 22 NCAA sports. Its member institutions are:

- University of Arizona

- Arizona State University

- University of California, Berkeley

- University of California, Los Angeles

- University of Colorado at Boulder

- University of Oregon

- Oregon State University

- University of Southern California

- Stanford University

- University of Utah

- University of Washington

- Washington State University

The roots of the Pac-12 go back to December 2, 1915, when the Pacific Coast Conference was founded at a meeting in Portland, Oregon. The Commissioner of the Conference is Larry Scott, previously Chairman and CEO of the Women's Tennis Association and a former professional tennis player himself. In July 2009, Scott replaced retiring Pac-10 Commissioner Thomas Hansen who had held the position for 26 years.

DANETTE LEIGHTON, CHIEF MARKETING OFFICER

Illustration 8.1 Danette Leighton

Danette Leighton became CMO of the Pac-12 Conference halfway through 2010 while it was still the Pac-10, brought in by its new Commissioner Larry Scott as part of his new executive team. Scott's business background and familiarity with marketing was a draw for Leighton, and she set about creating a new type of marketing team that could take the not-for-profit organizing governance body into a new era. According to Leighton, "Prior to Commissioner Scott's appointment, we were primarily a governance and administrative body. With Larry's background in professional sports, he has brought a new mix of talent to his executive team, primarily from pro-sports with a balance of long-time collegiate administration."

Leighton is the first-ever CMO for the organization because, "Larry felt the need to establish a marketing communications unit that didn't exist before," she says. Her responsibilities include leading the Conference in the development and implementation of strategic marketing and

Table 8.1   Danette Leighton professional experience

2010–current:	Chief Marketing Officer, Pac-12 Conference
2000–2010:	Vice President, Marketing and Brand Development Maloof Sports and Entertainment (NBA's Sacramento Kings, ARCO Arena and WNBA's Sacramento Monarchs)
1999–2000:	Sony Sports Marketing Division – PGA Tour and Sony Open in Hawaii

communications programs, as well as integrating and supporting the marketing interests of the member institutions.

Leighton calls it "a marketer's dream" because she is getting the opportunity to develop a marketing team from scratch but with an established brand. "Most people are familiar with the Pac-12, its long-standing tradition of both competitive excellence and academic excellence. It's just one of those conferences that hasn't necessarily pounded its chest enough," she says.

Coincidentally, Leighton began her career in sports marketing as a PR intern at the Pac-10. More recently she spent ten years as VP of marketing and brand development for Maloof Sports and Entertainment, where she oversaw all branding and marketing efforts for the NBA Sacramento Kings, ARCO Arena, and the overall business operations for the WNBA Sacramento Monarchs, so she has been able to bring the pro-sports marketing expertise to the Pac-12, albeit in a scaled-back form. "I had some idea of the structure that I needed. It's a Conference office, a small group, so I really needed to make sure that the staff was very strong and kind of Jack-of-all-trades because they would be touching so many parts of the business. You don't have the luxury of having a big team so you need to have a really solid group of people," said Leighton.

She inherited three internal positions that were already working with Commissioner Scott as the Business Development Team. They were alumni of member universities, two of whom had just graduated – one from business school, and they were "total go-getters" wanting to learn everything. The business development team leads the data mining for the group, including establishing methodologies for the team and providing the analytics for projects and campaigns.

Leighton also inherited a long-term PR/sports information position which she strengthened by creating a media relations group that could manage everything on the field and on the court, looking for proactive story lines across the sports. This team of four divides the sports between them to cover the breadth of play.

Her first hire was a senior director of marketing, with a background in creative which is one of the things Leighton felt was missing. She brought in someone from the NBA with whom she had previously worked quite closely, and who could look at everything from design creative to enhancing events. "Her role is to do everything to enhance all of our championships – to look through a different lens across market promotions, PSA campaigns, and to develop a look and feel of the image behind the Conference," says Leighton.

She then hired a VP of public affairs because she felt strongly that there was a significant need for off-the-court, off-the-field PR and marketing assistance, and under that umbrella, she incorporated a new digital resource, hiring someone from the NFL. Since the new digital media manager has come on board, the organization has relaunched a new website, kick-started a presence in the social media world, and set about growing a database through database marketing.

Leighton's job is to enhance the visibility of the Pac-12 overall, so the small team works closely across common goals whether it's to promote the Conference brand or its individual brands (institutions). For example, Leighton's team may help the University of Washington create a story that could be of national media interest which helps the Pac-12 overall. "We do a lot of that because holistically as a unit we are very strong and we can go out there and market our individual brands across which there are so many stories that are authentic and of interest to the media. It's the simple reminder that all of these 12 brands play under one umbrella," according to Leighton.

The Conference wants students to attend its universities and it aims to attract student athletes as well as letting the general student know about its universities so that when they and their parents are making decisions on where they want to attend to get a higher education, its institutions are top of mind. The number one objective, though, is the student athlete experience. "We're always looking to make sure that the student athlete has the best academic and athletic experience they possibly can have because we recognize that not everyone will have the benefit of going pro. In many cases the collegiate experience is the pinnacle of most of our student athletes' careers," says Leighton.

One of the most important roles the Conference plays in furthering the interest in the sports and the athletes is the negotiation of media rights. Most of the deals are decade-long agreements, so significant decisions are in the hands of Commissioner Scott and his executive team as they enter discussions in the next year. "At the end of the day, we're a content provider of major events and championships, and this generates revenue for the institutions along with ticket sales and sponsorship," according to Leighton.

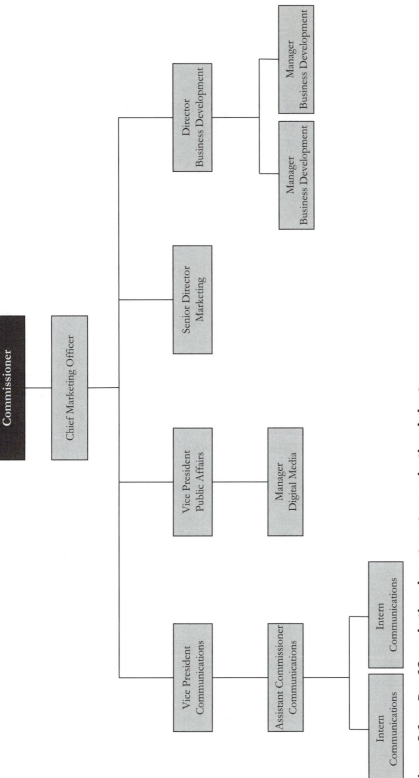

Figure 8.1   Pac-12 marketing department organizational chart

Like many CMOs, Leighton needs to deliver on the short-term objectives each academic year, but she also needs to address longer-term goals. One of the first initiatives Commissioner Scott undertook when he came on board was to commission some research to help define brand pillars to differentiate the organization from other conferences. Leighton refers to this as "essentially our brand Bible" with the three key pillars being about west coast, innovation, and excellence. She tries to bring this to life in her team's everyday efforts, but she also is creating specific programs to underline these values. For example, she recognized an East Coast bias when it comes to West Coast sports, so one of the biggest initiatives last year was to bring Pac-10 coaches to New York for a media day, including a trip to Bristol, Connecticut, to visit ESPN – allowing sports commentators to personally interact and get to know them. Relationships were established and now, every time one of the Pac-12's teams are on ESPN, the talent will recall meeting the coach and Commissioner Scott, crediting the Pac-12 for change.

It is early days for Leighton, but KPIs already are important as she continues to develop her team. Her benchmarks range from how successful events are in terms of attendance and media attention to specific metrics around special initiatives such as the coaches tour. And while she looks to enhance team delivery, she does so against a backdrop of minimal resources. "Resources are our people, our manpower, our institutions, and what's happening in higher education as a whole. Everyone is challenged financially and so it's a lot of work. I have a lot of respect for what each of our athletic departments has to do when you know that some of our schools are sponsoring over 30 sports," states Leighton.

The Pac-12 is backed by a relatively small team of around 40 which includes a sports management group, a compliance group, governance and administration, and the marketing unit. Internal communications within the Conference is primarily through the executive team, led by Commissioner Scott, but as a membership body, the Conference also regularly meets with its member institutions' CEOs, athletic directors, faculty athletic representatives, and coaches. Conference calls occur on a regular basis with these groups, and according to Leighton, "We're always online communicating with our members, so we do a lot of decision making with these key groups in real time." The way the structure is set up, decisions require membership votes, so the organization works like a democracy.

Given its heritage, Commissioner Scott, Leighton, and the executive team represent major change agents to the organization. According to Leighton, "I think we are bringing a more private sector mindset to what was more of a public sector business. The biggest change for this organization is blending and evolving – maintaining the tradition and heritage, and protecting the governance aspect, blending that with knowledge and skills from the private sector to build sustainability, look at opportunities for growth, and determine how to generate more revenue for member institutions without completely commercializing the organization."

Given the Pac-12's key brand pillars and its western base, and given what the west stands for, Leighton harkens to a pioneering spirit behind the organization and its new leadership. There's also an opportunity as the Conference expands its sights to attract students from Asia and the Pacific Rim, which is one of its longer-term goals.

With her communications beginnings, what did Leighton bring to the Pac-12 that a more classically trained marketer might not have? "I think I have an awareness of the strength and the power of public relations because I've experienced it firsthand. I've seen the evolution of what's occurred with media but then I also have the benefit of spending the majority of my life putting butts in seats, generating revenue, meeting a bottom line, and thinking about how we get the latest, the greatest, and the newest to compete more effectively. And I understand the balance of both. More than anything in this day and age, I understand you have to be real because your consumers and fans can see right through you," she says. "For someone like me, I don't know how to be anything but real and transparent and if I had to do that, I wouldn't do well at my job."

9 The Responsible CMO: IBM

International Business Machines (IBM) is an American multi-national computer, technology, business consulting, and IT consulting corporation headquartered in Armonk, New York. IBM is one of the few information technology companies with a continuous history dating back to the nineteenth century. The company manufactures and sells computer hardware and software, with a focus on the latter, and offers infrastructure services, hosting services, and consulting services in areas ranging from mainframe computers to nanotechnology. IBM has been well known through most of its recent history as the world's largest computer company and systems integrator. IBM has 406,000 employees in 173 countries, and holds more patents than any other US-based technology company.

JON IWATA, SENIOR VICE PRESIDENT, MARKETING AND COMMUNICATIONS

The catalyst for Jon Iwata's rise to lead IBM's marketing team worldwide in July 2008, was not about gaining efficiencies, but rather IBM CEO Sam Palmisano was looking to enhance the effectiveness of the function across two aspects: external and internal. Externally, it became logical to Palmisano that IBM needed to speak with one voice across every constituent that mattered

Table 9.1   Jon Iwata professional experience

2008–current:	Senior Vice President, Marketing and Communications, IBM
2002–2008:	Senior Vice President, Communications, IBM
1995–2002:	Vice President, Corporate Communications, IBM
1989–1995:	IBM Corporate Headquarters
1984–1989:	IBM, Almaden Research Center, Silicon Valley

Illustration 9.1 Jon Iwata

to the company. But, as Iwata points out, "It went beyond that because you don't need to structurally integrate organizations to have simple message alignment and consistency." He adds, "I think the deeper point here is that you have so much information being shared and known about corporations across every segment that the ability to segment audience and message is almost impossible. So you have to approach the marketplace fully, and that's not just customers but also shareholders, employees, governments, and all the rest. We have to start from the premise that that's the way you have to engage holistically, fully integrated, across all constituents. And therefore we needed to not just put the things together but in fact create a different kind of team."

The internal aspect of the realignment was related to the transparency and visibility of what goes on inside the organization. Iwata believes that the actual behavior of the company, the culture, and the performance cannot be managed as if they were separate from the outside reality that can be projected through brand management or public relations or advertising. Iwata states, "So your culture and your external reputation and brand need to be managed holistically as well."

The consolidation of sorts didn't involve hiring in as much as changes were made conceptualizing the kind of expertise that was required in the combined functions. Iwata provides two examples: "The IBM brand is respected, well known and has value, but in terms of how our brands were managed, we had a brand management function. But the reality of what goes on inside of an organization is going to have tremendous bearing on the brand or how the company is perceived. Meanwhile, the management of culture was managed by internal communications or organizational behavior, completely separate from those who worry about the brand. So we put them together into a new construct so the people who focus on corporate culture and those who focus on brand meaning are together on one team which we call the IBM Brand System. So corporate culture and brand management are fused together."

The second example Iwata explains, "We've also changed our market research function. We're not just doing market research but now we're pressing much more into analyzing data and information not just to understand the marketplace better but to create intellectual capital that actually can be deployed with clients. It's almost like our analytics group; it's also most like the marketing R&D group. There has been an evolution of the so-called 'market intelligence' group from market research to marketing R&D."

In addition to creating a "different type of team," Iwata talks of bringing more science and rigor, analytics, and technology to the way the company launches products and services through the "IBM Demand System." Likening it to an integrated supply chain operation approach as a parallel example, he describes how IBM takes aspects such as advertising, promotion, PR, sales, collateral, and the like, as individual pieces that his team are working to make more coherent alongside analytics and technology so that it's much more of a value creation option.

71

The IBM marketing approach is a matrix. One part of the matrix is the three profit and loss (P&L) BUs: the hardware business, software business, and services business. Marketing communications staffs are attached to each of these big P&L units. The second part of the matrix is geographic. IBM goes to market geographically. The third part of the matrix is the corporate function where discipline leaders sit and where, it seems, best practice is fostered through professional excellence. Each profession or discipline has a leader who ensures the quality of the profession regardless of where the staff member reports – P&L BU, geography, or corporate. Iwata provides an example: "External relations and analyst relations is led by Ed Barbini. There are hundreds of people who are in external relations who are either in the P&L units or they're all over the world in the countries. They may report into the country or report into the software group but as professionals, they look to Ed Barbini as the guy who sets the standards, who ensures the quality of the profession, and who probably will be responsible for their jobs somewhere in the world. So we have the value or attributes of centralization because you've got centralization of the professional skills groups but they are attached to the organizational structure of the company."

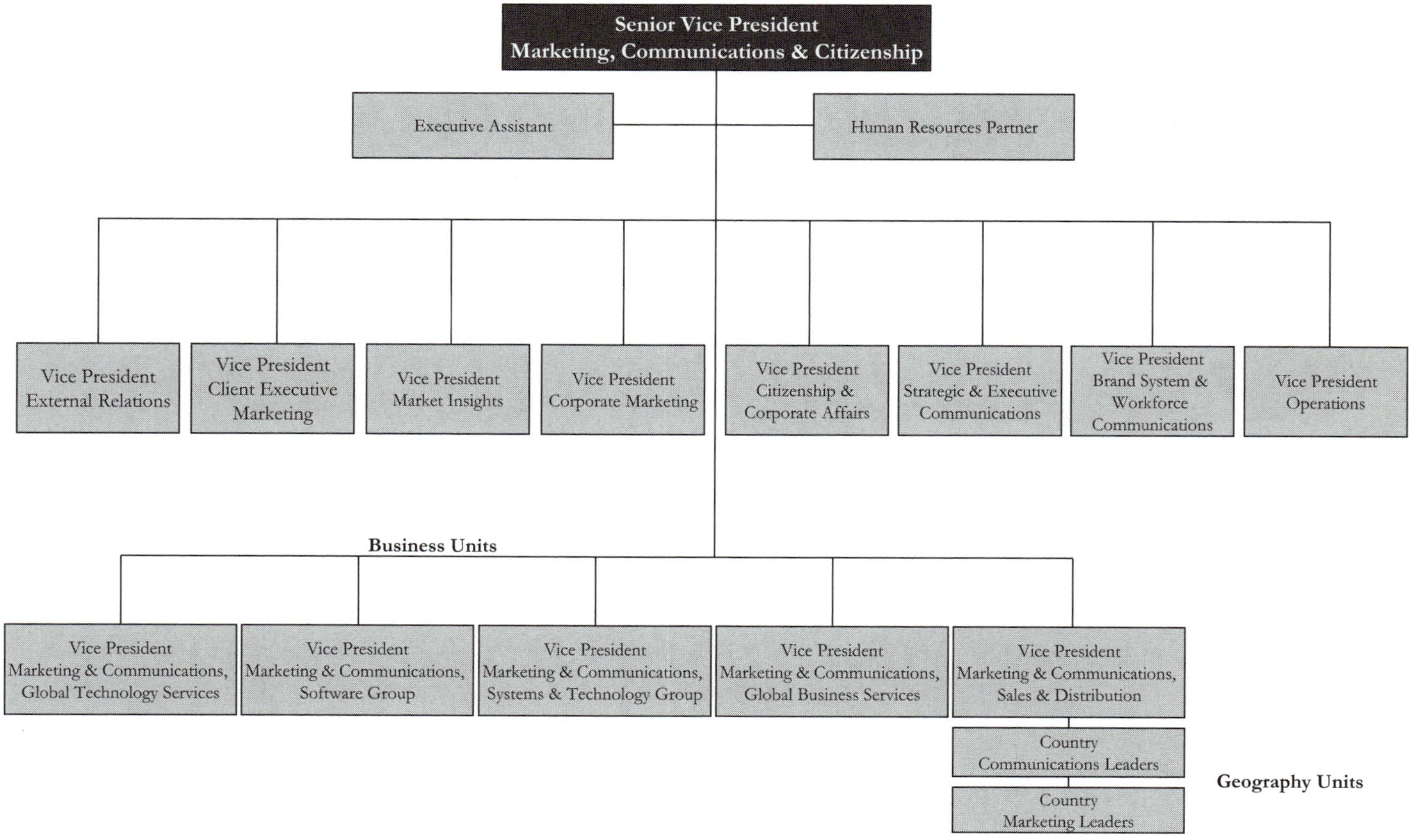

Senior Vice President
Marketing, Communications & Citizenship

Executive Assistant

Human Resources Partner

Vice President External Relations

Vice President Client Executive Marketing

Vice President Market Insights

Vice President Corporate Marketing

Vice President Citizenship & Corporate Affairs

Vice President Strategic & Executive Communications

Vice President Brand System & Workforce Communications

Vice President Operations

Business Units

Vice President Marketing & Communications, Global Technology Services

Vice President Marketing & Communications, Software Group

Vice President Marketing & Communications, Systems & Technology Group

Vice President Marketing & Communications, Global Business Services

Vice President Marketing & Communications, Sales & Distribution

Geography Units

Country Communications Leaders

Country Marketing Leaders

Figure 9.1   IBM marketing communications and citizenship

Professional disciplines include external relations, brand management, market management, market intelligence, demand management, corporate citizenship, and operations. Iwata approximates 300 people sitting at the corporate discipline level. Then there are probably 2,500 marketing staff in the P&Ls, and another 2,500 in the countries.

From a planning perspective, IBM has two cycles. According to Iwata, "I make this very simple. We have a strategic set of planning cycles and we have a budgeting cycle. The strategic starts first. We call that a spring plan which focuses on strategic priorities such as how we will shift to grow, what aspects we need to downplay, what aspects we need to elevate, any sort of geographic shift, business line shift, skill set solutions. We set our priorities. And then we follow that with fiscal or budget cycle which is in the fall, and all that gets reconciled with the economic and financial targets of the corporation. This also has to be reconciled with each of the P&Ls and with each of the countries so that goes top down, bottom up, back and forth until we're all tired out. That's at the tectonic plate level annually."

Iwata also makes the point that quarterly checks are done, priorities are revisited and adjusted if need be with regard to competition, messaging, and the portfolio. Additionally, he focuses on talent – constantly moving people to broaden their careers, bringing people in, moving people around the world. He calls this "collective talent management."

Planning with agency partners mirrors the company planning process. Iwata says, "The agency is mapped to the spring and fall plan. They get a sense of our priorities and see the budgets. Day-to-day they are integrated with us and our go-to-market activities and our campaigns. We've consolidated our agency relationships to a smaller number of mostly global firms both in PR and in advertising and events. And therefore they are fully integrated with our operations and, for the most part, they have been for over ten years, in some cases over 15 years."

KPIs are many. At the corporate level, Iwata and his team pay a lot of attention to the state of the IBM brand which is measured in many different ways across many different peer groups. In terms of the products and services, the KPIs there include market share; how IBM is perceived against the competition; client engagement, satisfaction, referenceability, ease of doing business with, and value for money. Client-related measurements are very much related to share performance, share of wallet, share of mind, and share of industry pie. And then there is "a whole bunch of internal measurements, which we care about very much," according to Iwata.

As Iwata's marketing team continues to develop newer disciplines, he's looking to continue to build and expand include social media, analytics, marketing automation, and a continued roll-out of brand and culture management. And while there has been a historic shift towards digital in recent years, Iwata talks of the shift within digital towards Web 2.0 from Web 1.0. "Call it social media and we're investing heavily in it both in terms of what we do as well as policy and management systems that are working to social media. Within analytics, we're looking to build technology as well as a skill set. We need people who understand, who have questions to ask, and know what tools we need to make sense of all of the data available to us. In terms of marketing automation, that's a roll-out of tools in how to use them to change the process of the work of marketing to increase effectiveness. And of course the brand and culture management which we call brand system doesn't so much require investment but rather a new skill set that we have to support."

The employee piece becomes even more important when one considers the sheer people power that 406,000 staff can have. According to Iwata, "We're deploying more and more employees to use social media in our business interest. Internally, it's almost 100 percent of the population but externally it's up to several thousand. Our goal is to create a policy environment for education and the tools and technologies so that 100 percent of the employee population feels confident and expert at using social media for business purposes. That's our goal."

There are over 200,000 IBMers registered with IBM profiles on Facebook, and about the same on LinkedIn. Iwata says, "In both cases, we're the largest professional populations. So we already have about half of the work force already heavily into social media. The question isn't whether they're using social media. The question is how can we help them use social media responsibly and to help IBM's business interest. And that's kind of the goal of our social media efforts."

Did Iwata see any disadvantages coming to a marketing leadership role from largely a communications background? He says, "The challenges included a complete lack of familiarity with the vocabulary of marketing. I'd call it the orthodox use of marketing. I have no formal background in marketing, so that's everything from the funnel to the basket to the four Ps, to all of the IBM unique jargon that the marketing organization uses around our tools and processes to execute marketing work. So in that regard, it was a different tribe. But I also think that the challenge wasn't a different mindset, and I'm going to bridge to the advantages of coming at this from a PR or communications background. We're in a mindset historically within marketing which makes total sense by the way. Marketing's job is to market the products and services of the company. The corporate communications job is about having an understanding that we have to think about all of the audiences and constituents that matter to us or that we matter to them. So you don't do anything without thinking about how it will be understood or received by the different audiences – including media, management, staff, retirees, unions, communities, suppliers, customers, and so on. This is second nature, but not to marketers. But in the world in which we're moving, people care about the where the product was made, they care about the behavior of the company executives, or how the company is treating its employees, and they know who is answering the telephone when they call for customer service. And you can't, as marketers, say 'I don't want to pay attention to that, I simply want to talk to you about why you should prefer my products'."

Iwata continues, "The heritage of public relations and communications has trained us to take a multi-audience, multi-stakeholder view, a multi-dimensional view of what we do. And I think that has been a good thing. But the traditional model of marketing, as my colleagues in marketing would first point out, is really breaking down. Everything from the funnel to traditional advertising is all breaking down so they are much more open to ideas and approaches."

10 The Creative CMO: Adobe Systems Incorporated

Founded in 1982, Adobe Systems Incorporated is an American computer software company headquartered in San Jose, California. The company has historically focused upon the creation of multi-media and creativity software products, with a more-recent foray towards rich Internet application software development. Adobe acquired its former competitor, Macromedia, in 2005, which added newer software products and platforms such as Coldfusion, Dreamweaver, Flash, and Flex to its product portfolio, and then acquired Omniture, an online marketing and web analytics company, in 2009.

ANN LEWNES, SENIOR VICE PRESIDENT, GLOBAL MARKETING

Illustration 10.1   Ann Lewnes

Table 10.1   Ann Lewnes professional experience

2006–current:	Senior Vice President, Global Marketing, Adobe Systems Incorporated
1985–2006:	Vice President, Marketing, Intel Corporation (her first four years were in Intel's corporate communications group)

Ann Lewnes is responsible for Adobe's corporate brand and integrated marketing efforts worldwide. She drives the company's corporate positioning, branding and identity, PR, marketing campaigns, field marketing, and education segment marketing to ensure strong connections with customers and constituents. As champion of Adobe's brand to employees and the community, she also oversees Adobe's internal communications and community relations efforts including the Adobe Foundation, which funds philanthropic initiatives around the world.

When she arrived in 2006, she inherited a structure that already included all of the communications functions whether it was corporate communications, PR, analyst relations, employee communications, and CSR alongside all of the traditional marketing functions. The one piece of marketing that she did not inherit was regional marketing responsibility, which previously sat in sales, but Lewnes felt that in order to be a more cohesive and global organization, she needed responsibility for that as well so regional marketing moved under her remit in 2009.

The marketing group has a campaign-centric approach so the business is segmented. "For a company of our size," says Lewnes, "we're extremely diversified, probably on the order of a Microsoft believe it or not considering how big they are and given that they are in so many businesses. We're in a lot of businesses, too, so the way we have handled that is to segment our audiences and then we have comprehensive campaigns spanning everything from PR all the way to our website. And we organize those by segments."

Marketing is fairly centralized as well at Adobe. According to Lewnes, "Around the world, we have one big marketing organization." The only aspect that does not report directly to Lewnes is Adobe product marketing organizations, but she oversees a marketing council which includes folks from product marketing in the BUs, so she has "shared authority" for all business marketing. So while product marketers report directly to their BU leaders, they have dotted lines to Lewnes. In that way, Lewnes' central marketing group effectively manages all of the marketing working in partnership with the BUs.

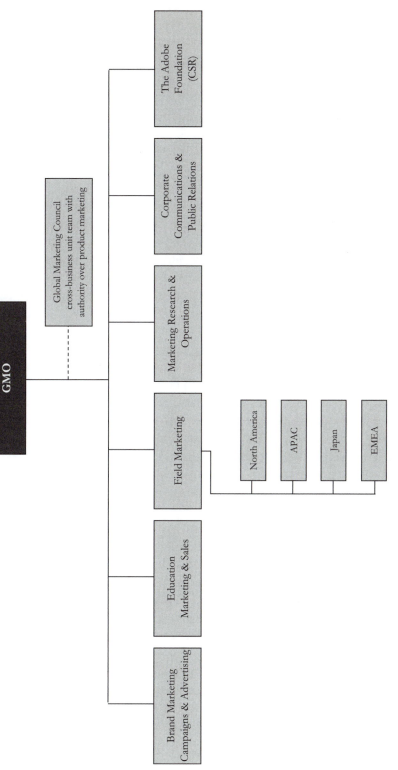

Figure 10.1   Adobe global marketing organizational chart

The group reporting directly to Lewnes numbers over 400 employees worldwide. The number of BU marketing employees is much smaller. Despite owning the entire marketing mix, one of her biggest challenges is unifying the master brand voice. "We have businesses that have been rather distinct from one another, so they all want to have their own kind of campaign, and if we're not careful, we get siloed and fragmented," she says. So one of her priorities is unifying all of the different campaigns to ensure that Adobe, the master brand, gets credit for the breadth of products and solutions on offer rather than focus on individual products which fragments the Adobe message.

Previous planning methodologies were fragmented as well and the marketing team didn't necessarily have a voice, so Lewnes and her team have worked on evolving the process into a smoother, more aligned approach. "It's a pretty rigorous process which is based on revenue goals and alignment of BU leadership, sales, and marketing. And the marketing basically acts as the mechanism for the sales force to meet the revenue goals," says Lewnes. "Now we have a much tighter process and I think there has to be alignment before we basically are comfortable proceeding."

Agency partnership is tight as well. Agency partners are managed exclusively through Lewnes' organization – another change she made on her arrival at Adobe. Two major partners are involved in the planning stages: the AOR for advertising and AOR for PR. The former acts as Adobe's major creative partner globally, although other agencies book media for Adobe in various markets around the world. The global PR partner acts as US AOR and covers some but not all markets outside the US.

One over-riding aspect of planning is creativity. As Lewnes says, "We're Adobe, so our business is creativity. Creativity has a lot to do with our DNA. It's really important for us to role model and I think that as an organization there are a number of ways that we do that." She aspires for the organization to have world-class marketing and claims that Adobe spends a lot of time on the quality of its communication. "There is an amazing amount of attention to detail and not only are we focused on messaging but we're extremely focused on the experience that we are giving to our customers. Our whole mission here is around digital experiences and making those world class. So when we create a campaign, it's very experiential. Most of our money is spent on web marketing. In fact, 75 percent of our money is spent on some form of web marketing whether its social, display advertising, relationship marketing, or our website which is one of the most trafficked in the world with 350 million unique visitors per month making us one of the largest corporate websites in the world."

As just one example of internal creativity, Lewnes expresses pride over a program recently implemented which has been tremendously successful called "The Seeds of Innovation," an idea which originated from Adobe's head of Asia Pacific marketing. The concept is simple: a biannual competition where marketing employees around the world are invited to submit ideas that they would like to see implemented at Adobe. Lewnes' staff internationally reviews all of the entries – they had 38 in the most recent round – and selects one winner. That winner is awarded $100,000 to implement their program. It's an idea which has gotten a lot of traction, says Lewnes, because there are programs that would never happen unless they were able to put forth the thinking in this sort of format. The most recent winner was an optimization to Adobe's trial download process. The number one factor in terms of driving purchase for products is whether the customer downloads a trial piece of software from the website. There is a huge correlation between that and ultimate purchase, so the winning idea was a methodology for optimizing that trial process such that Adobe could increase the conversion rate between trial and purchase. It was a very innovative way to do it, and the winner has been funded to implement the project.

Against this creative backdrop, how is success measured? Lewnes breaks it down into two pieces: "We have metrics around loyalty for our product and loyalty for our brand. We use a variety of traditional brand metrics, and we use some third-party metrics. For instance, the Interbrand's annual ranking. When I arrived, we were not on that list. Last year for the first time we were on the top 100, at 95. This year our goal was to move up by 10 percent and we're now number 88. We also use the Brand Asset® Valuator. We do internal brand tracking and an annual customer loyalty study. We have a variety of different vectors that we measure customers' satisfaction and ultimately there's a loyalty index that we've developed."

Lewnes believes that one has to prove the value of marketing "every single day." She works with her group to provide justification and substantiation for everything they do. And she's thankful for measurement tools: "We care so much about measurement that we bought Omniture because we want to have that capability in-house. The creation of content, the measurement of content, and the delivery of content is all on one continuum now. And so the nirvana that we've all been waiting for is the ability to actually measure all the stuff that we put out into the marketplace, and now we can do that."

Lewnes also has responsibility for the marketing research organization within Adobe, and she reports a breadth of different surveys undertaken by that group which feeds into the whole marketing planning process. This group also is responsible for the company's marketing automation systems, digital asset management, and contact management systems.

In addition to her traditional marketing responsibilities, Lewnes is also responsible for the education segment of Adobe's business, which is a half-billion-dollar business. Although unusual for a CMO to have a P&L role, it made the most sense given Adobe's portfolio of business. The company markets enterprise products to its B2B customers, and it sells a lot of software to both small businesses as well as enterprise-level business. It has a B2C business as well, but it's not as large as the B2B segment. A third constituent is the education market which is Adobe's largest vertical segment selling K through 12 (kindergarten through twelfth grade high school) as well as higher education, but also to individual students who are increasingly big users of creative software. "Creative software is basically becoming required to do any type of class work and it's increasingly important as you move into the workforce. Everybody needs to be able to use photographic software, make videos and create websites, so there is a kind of standard of communication skills moving into the twenty-first century. So we sell a lot of software into the educational segment as well," says Lewnes.

Lewnes inherited the education segment because collective wisdom was that the education business needed to transcend all of the other businesses and reside somewhere in corporate. "It's one of the most exciting parts of my role because education is something that the company is extremely passionate about," she says. Hand-in-hand with education, the Adobe Foundation, which also falls under Lewnes' responsibilities, has a flagship program called Youth Voices, an educational program where Adobe supplies software, curriculum, and mentors to kids in underserved communities in 50 countries. "We help them create largely documentary and photographic essays about experiences that they're having and it's one of the most humbling, inspiring, exciting things that we do," according to Lewnes.

Looking forward, Lewnes points to digital's continued evolution as a next chapter for Adobe even though the company is already deeply engaged. "We made a right-hand turn probably two years ago to really double down on digital marketing. So I'm not sure how much more we could move to the web quite frankly because we're pretty much almost all in. But what we're doing on the web continues to evolve considerably," according to Lewnes. The next frontier seems to be social as it relates to PR. "We're finding a tremendous shift in terms of PR in particular; social as becoming PR. I'm pretty sure that press releases as we know them will go away and nobody will be happier than me. I think those kinds of traditional methods are somewhat obsolete. A tweet or a posting on any one of the social sites like Facebook, or comments that somebody makes about you on C-NET, Mashable, or Digg have so much more weight than what you say about yourself," says Lewnes. So she claims that she and her team are looking at a total transformation over to social in terms of communication.

She continues, "Is a Facebook posting a marketing technique or is it PR? Well, it's both. Is a tweet PR or marketing technique? Well, it's both. And I think this has become a convergence that I think has happened so quickly and so dramatically that we're all trying to catch up even at a company like Adobe where it's kind of our business. It's transformational, completely transformational."

Lewnes cannot fathom how functions could continue to be separated because "they are so inextricably linked and blended now that I don't see how that could work but I guess different strokes for different folks. I don't see how it could work for us."

The importance of digital and social media becomes even more acute when Lewnes considers the global marketplace. "I think that the world has become a very small place and we have to adapt ourselves accordingly. Regionally, Adobe has been a pretty North America-focused company and the markets have exploded for our types of technology worldwide, so I think a global focus is much more important for us. Social plays a big role in that. One bad review, one comment from an executive about your company changes everything, and you need to be responsive in a way that you never were before. You need 24-hour customer support; you need people who are talented at moving quickly analyzing results. It's just a totally different game," according to Lewnes.

How has Lewnes' original experience in editorial and corporate communications at Intel served her in her marketing roles? "What I think really helped me was that incredible foundation in the ability to communicate clearly and articulately about products, about the company itself. Your most important skill is being able to communicate clearly verbally and through written form, and I don't think that's going to change. Your ability to message something, to really think through what is the value of this thing I'm trying to sell, what is the proposition," according to Lewnes.

Did she have to learn anything new? "Completely," she replies, "Along with the communication skills, you need analytical skills. We have a lot of people that we hire now who are web analysts or database analysts or search marketing professionals that provide totally different skill sets than traditional marketing and PR professionals. And even when hiring younger people, we look for social media expertise."

11 The Mobile CMO: Nissan Motor Co., Ltd.

Nissan Motor Company, Ltd is a multi-national automaker headquartered in Japan. It was formerly a core member of the Nissan Group, but has become more independent after its restructuring under CEO Carlos Ghosn. It formerly marketed vehicles under the "Datsun" brand name and is one of the largest car manufacturers in the world. In 1999, Nissan entered into a two-way alliance with Renault S.A. of France, which owns 44.4 percent of Nissan while Nissan holds 15 percent of Renault shares, as of 2008. The Renault–Nissan Alliance, which was established in March 1999, was the first industrial and commercial partnership of its kind involving a French and a Japanese company.

SIMON SPROULE, CORPORATE VICE PRESIDENT, GLOBAL MARKETING COMMUNICATIONS

Illustration 11.1   **Simon Sproule**

Table 11.1   Simon Sproule professional experience

2010–current:	Corporate Vice President, Global Marketing Communications, Nissan Motor Co., Ltd. (Yokohama, Japan)
2009–2010:	Director, Communications, Renault–Nissan Alliance (Paris, France)
2009:	Corporate Vice President, Communications, Microsoft Corporation
2004–2009:	Corporate Vice President, Global Communications, Nissan Motor Co., Ltd.
2003–2004:	Vice President, Corporate Communications, Nissan North America
2001–2003:	Vice President, Communications, Aston Martin Jaguar Land Rover North America
2000–2001:	Vice President, Communications, Jaguar North America
1998–2000:	Manager, Communications, Truck Vehicle Center, Ford Motor Company
1996–1998:	Manager, Corporate Affairs, Ford of Britain Public Affairs
1994–1996:	Press Officer, Ford of Britain Public Affairs

When Simon Sproule returned to Nissan from the Renault–Nissan Alliance where he was global communications director, it was to take up the reins of a new global marketing organization set up by Renault–Nissan CEO Carlos Ghosn to whom Sproule reported as the Renault–Nissan global communications director and before that as corporate VP for Global Communications for Nissan.

In addition to increasing collaboration between the marketing disciplines, the move was as much about collaboration with the product planning cycle. According to Sproule, "We deliberately made the move to interact with the product planning and business strategy functions because we wanted to get into a position where there was a seamless flow from customer research through product development, right the way through to the end consumer, which is quite unique because one of the things we're doing is that you have soup to nuts all in one group."

Sproule reported directly to Ghosn for seven years, and says he still has a very direct link with him, but he now reports to Andy Palmer, SVP for global planning and program management in a deliberate move to create a closer connection to marketing and product.

In a similar move, Renault announced Stephen Norman as SVP, global marketing and communications. Previously SVP of global marketing, Renault has taken a parallel decision to combine marketing and communications.

According to Sproule, "The turning point for the reorganization of function started when Ghosn asked a simple question: How can we manage our brand better? He wanted to know if we were doing everything we could to maximize how our brands were presented and how we were spending our marketing dollars."

The journey took about a year and Sproule got marketers and communicators from both brands together to work it through beyond the politics and the turf battles. He and his team studied automotive and non-automotive brands, looking at best-in-class integration. And he says, "We rapidly came to this conclusion that unless we forced integration through organizational change, it just would not happen. We would never get the depth of integration that is going to unlock the true potential. We knew that if we were going to drive change, deep and long term, then integration was the only way to get it right." Sproule continues, "I think we are ahead of the game. We're not pioneers, but we're ahead of the game in terms of the automotive industry."

Central to the combining of forces under the marketing umbrella, Sproule lists three elements which are critical to building a great brand, regardless of industry, "First and foremost, you have to have a great product. Without that, game over. Second, you have to have a great customer experience. For us, that means loyalty. Repurchase ratio is key – do people like buying the car and do they love owning it? Third is building a clear and consistent position for the brand so that people understand who you are. You can do it on the first two alone, but if you have sub-par communications, ultimately people are not going to understand your brand, the picture will be confused, and you'll eventually conclude that you need all three."

Within his marketing organization, Sproule has global marketing, global brands, global communication, investor relations, CSR, and internal communications. These are seen as the building blocks of the function. He also has a group of individuals who have product upstream or product management responsibility so that he can be more involved in how Nissan products contribute to the brand.

Sproule has some 150–175 employees in his central marketing team, but a broader group of more than 500 in the regions. Nissan is structured into three regions: Americas; Europe, Middle East, Africa and India; and Asia Pacific. Each of the regions has its own marketing communications operations, and

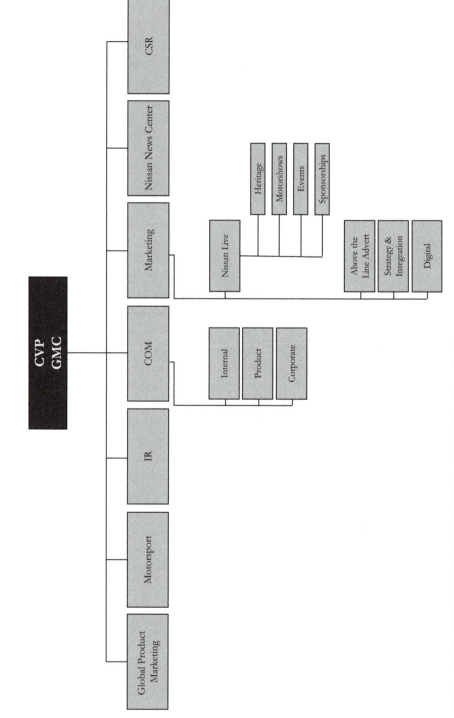

Figure 11.1   Nissan global marketing communications chart

Sproule admits that, "Historically, we have been a company that tended to have quite strong regional independence, so that's part of the reason I think we have ended up with a brand that's not as well-regarded as it should be given the quality of our product. So the journey that we are undertaking now is to build a much more collegiate integrated working relationship with the regions, so that they feel part of the bigger global picture and that they have the ability to influence global decisions. At the same time, we globally have a bigger role and more influence with the regions so it cuts both ways."

It's early days for Sproule, but he is already looking for some early wins. For the first time, marketing and communications at the global level is integrating on budget parameters. "We will make our decisions based on the quality of the ideas and not on the traditional 'well marketing always spent this' and 'PR always spent that'," says Sproule. "I think it will work because what we are doing is holding a mirror up to the organization," he says. "And I think the incentive for people to work together will come from how the process is managed and how people feel. They have got to have independence and freedom. With any big organizational change, the natural reflex is skepticism, followed by how this is going to impact me and then it's about proving that it's going to be useful. We are going through that learning at the moment. I think that if we can show that we make life easier for everybody both in the center and in the regions through better strategic planning and more mature conversations about resource allocation, then we will actually be able to do more collectively, reinvest in new activity and achieve greater results."

Sproule chairs quarterly planning meetings which include Nissan's global AOR, TBWA\Chiat\Day. In the other marketing disciplines, there are no global AORs, however Sproule suspects that "ultimately, we will probably go looking for a global PR agency on the strategic rather than tactical level."

He's quick to point to new developments, too, as part of the new organization. "We're setting up a couple of initiatives which are part of the integration move. One is being called Nissan Live which is effectively integrating all of the event-based activities we undertake which include auto shows, sponsorships, and any sort of event where we speak directly with a human being," says Sproule who is looking at "Live" to deliberately create events that have multiple stakeholder audiences "as opposed to having one event over here for media or an event over there for customers or yet another event for investors." This is about driving some consistency in how Nissan presents the brand while at the same time maximizing investment. "We're also setting up a news center or 'content factory' where we are going to create our own stories which will then be funneled through a variety of different channels," he adds.

On the digital side it's very similar. "I would say it's probably even more critical on the digital side because that truly is global," Sproule says. "Fundamentally, digital is everywhere and it's on all of the time. And we know for a fact that consumers in one market will research a car if they know it sells in other markets. We can't do anything without somebody finding out about it which is absolutely right and that's the liberation of the Internet. It's a challenge for any brand."

Sproule and his team are tackling everything from applications to social media to website development and "everything in between" so that Nissan doesn't have multiple messages that conflict about the same product. He's also keen to apply some rigor and discipline in terms of central direction, individual markets, regions, and operations so that local markets don't do their own thing where you "suddenly find out that you've got ten different suppliers and you've got 30 different Facebook sites with Nissan in the name, and that's the situation we're in right now."

He sees an early win specifically in the area of digital development. "We're moving quite fast to get our hands around that because everyone is getting excited about developing apps for everything under the sun," says Sproule. "We are saying 'wait a minute guys. We can probably help you here and save you a lot of money.' We really like the idea of apps, but we want them to make sense and complement each other, not be random acts of marketing or communication kindness." He and his team are moving fairly fast to get a strategy in place, but he also recognizes that they have some maturing to do in the area.

In Japan, Nissan is ahead of the game in terms of its employee base. "We have our own internal social network which is accessible to some 20,000 employees in Japan, and our intention is to role that out globally. But when it comes to Facebook and other social media, we're still getting our hands around how to handle those, and I think we have some maturing to do with our strategy," Sproule says.

Nissan has social media guidelines globally for employees but Sproule admits that the guidelines are just basically common sense. "If you're going to write about the company, the industry or our competitors, whether you're doing it at home on a Sunday afternoon or from work on a Monday morning, there's no difference," he says.

Nissan also has been focusing more energy on getting employees into its products, recognizing that the workforce can provide the brand with its greatest ambassadors. Nissan's new LEAF™ electric car provides a perfect opportunity, says Sproule, "We have an active program to get employees into the new car to drive and experience it so that they can evangelize it with friends, neighbors, relatives, whoever. Previously, we have done this sort of thing informally, but this is now much more structured."

KPIs for Sproule's organization are many. He owns a number of KPIs of his own, and he also co-owns some KPIs with Nissan's head of sales or head of customer services. But the research function is part of Sproule's boss's group and not part of his direct resource, however he is a "customer" of the function. KPIs range from brand perception, transaction price and comparisons, product versus direct competition, customer service, loyalty, repurchase ratio, and external studies such as the Fortune 500.

Given that Sproule has come largely from a communications and therefore non-traditional marketing background, has he had to learn a new language? "Yes, and I probably will be learning for the rest of my life," he says. "I have been – in quotes – the PR guy through all of my career. And I think I have to address this issue. Whether you have a marketing guy or a PR guy taking over the integration function, whichever ways it falls there's always going to be people who are skeptical," he says.

Sproule is sanguine about the role and any skepticism: "My job is not to understand necessarily everything that everybody does. My job is air traffic control. I think that's where I'm going to spend most of my time. It's about ensuring that everyone knows what they are doing, working within the right framework, and making the right conversation at the right time. If I can get that to happen, I'll be satisified."

When Sproule's appointment was announced, he was interviewed by *PRWeek* and "all of the usual suspects" in his words. An interesting anecdote was that one British publication inteviewed a few PR people on Sproule's new role and the comments were almost universally negative. He says, "They felt that PR needs to be independent, that PR is different to marketing. I talked to the reporter afterwards and said that this is the classic kind of silo mentality that we don't need. I suggested that they ring up each one of those skeptics and ask them the basic question that if the CEO walked into their office and said I want you to become the head of marketing and PR for my company, will you do it?"

Sproule firmly believes that integration is the way of the future. "It's neither PR nor marketing coming into each other. It is the creation of a third discipline, a new profession as Jon Iwata (IBM) calls it," he says. "We are not eliminating PR. We are not eliminating marketing. There will be people who have specialized skills who will continue to operate in their universe and do it very well. But we have a need for a third type of individual who ultimately will become the norm rather than the exception, which will be people who are much more comfortable thinking in terms of integration and 360-degree communications as opposed to just thinking about marketing and PR."

Shortly after his appointment, Sproule gave a talk at an automotive PR industry function in the UK. "I told them that if you want to rise to the top of your profession, you ultimately need to become an integrationist. You need to become comfortable with dealing with all of these functions because that's the future for our profession. PR will still be strong and we'll still have a place at the table, but ultimately most big brands and most big organizations will go for integration. And I said that those people with those skills and who are comfortable in that environment will be the ones that achieve a career with the most success and mobility."

12 The Global Imperative

Big multi-national brands based in developed markets such as North America and Western Europe are increasing their focus and resources outside their home markets where growth potential is greatest versus the saturated and depressed western markets. According to *Advertising Age's* annual 100 Global Marketers report,[1] the US is home to only 5 percent of the world's population, however it accounts for 20 percent of global GDP and 34 percent of total worldwide advertising, making the US the largest ad market by far. But marketers in the US and other western markets are recognizing the opportunity to reach the remaining 95 percent of consumers in the world, and are shifting spend and resources accordingly. At the same time, brands from developing markets in Asia and Latin America are looking to tap into the lucrative west where consumers are more affluent and always looking for the next new thing despite being showered with choice already.

Regardless of their home base, CMOs will need to market where they see the most opportunity for growth and expansion. And aspects of an organization's social "graph" that is, how it engages with its audiences or its brand reputation will continue to transcend borders, making the global CMO role even more complex and challenging.

The results of EffectiveBrands' 2009 Leading Global Brands study,[2] which includes responses from some 21,500 global marketers who work on over 250-plus brands across all industries, indicated that getting the right balance between local versus global is a top challenge. Nearly 65 percent of respondents confirmed that global brands have become more important over the last five years. But only 15 percent fully agreed that their global

---

1   Advertising Age, 2010. *Top 100 Global Marketers*. [Online: December 6, 2010] Available at: http://adage.com [accessed: December 18, 2010].
2   Copyright: de Swaan Arons, M., van den Driest, F. 2010. *The Global Brand CEO*. EffectiveBrands' Leading Global Brands study.

brands were effectively leveraging scale. Even fewer marketers believed that their organizations excelled at quickly rolling out successful global brand initiatives.

The fact that the market is globalizing, according to Marc de Swaan Arons and Frank van den Driest in their book *The Global Brand CEO*, is probably the single biggest challenge for CMOs. Almost all of the things keeping marketers awake at night are connected to the global marketplace and going global. According to de Swaan Arons at a Marketing 50 summit in 2010, marketing used to be like bowling – lining up the pins and driving one big ball down the center of the alley to hit as many pins as possible. Today, global marketing is more like pinball. While one can exert some control on the flaps, there's a lot less control than a traditional marketer is accustomed to. Consumers and other important stakeholders have the control.

Brands also now operate in a fully transparent world where authenticity and relevance reign supreme. Nowhere is this more acute than in the digital and social media space. Despite language differences, the web represents the most global of all channels and as such, should be centrally-led or coordinated, at least from an organizing principle, to ensure consistency in brand image, messaging, and reputation. And if organizations haven't figured out their organizing principles yet, it will only get tougher to do so. Tom Friedman once said, "The World is Flat";[3] Mary Meeker of Morgan Stanley said that, "It's also increasingly in the palm of your hand."[4] Consumer and other important audiences are finding new ways to do old things faster and better than ever before, and more affordably, thanks to traditional innovators such as Apple, Google, and Amazon, as well as new innovators such as Facebook, Skype, Twitter, Hulu, and Zynga. Brands simply cannot afford to appear differently and have inconsistent messaging depending on the market.

Newer and more adept competition also presents a marketing leadership and organizational challenge, particularly for larger, more siloed organizations which are often slower to respond, let alone innovate.

One of the most challenging aspects for global marketers is around the role and responsibilities, which seem to vary widely from organization to organization in terms of the functions that report into marketing, the balance

---

3   Friedman, T.L. April 2005. *The World is Flat – A Brief History of the Twenty-First Century*, Farrar, Straus and Giroux.

4   Morgan Stanley Research, April 12, 2010. Internet Trends 2010 [Mary Meeker, called the "Queen of the Net" by Barron's in 1998, moved to venture capital firm Kleiner Perkins Caufield and Byers as a partner in November 2010].

between local and regional or global, and the level of connectivity with peers such as the chief financial officer and chief technical officer.

So what does all this mean for CMOs? The key questions around global marketing which seem to be rising to the top of the priority list for many CMOs include the following:

- What is the role of the center and the balance with regional marketing functions and efforts? Where do the solid reporting lines work? Where should dotted reporting lines be implemented? Is a matrix an appropriate structure? What is the right mechanism and balance for collaboration and institutionalizing best practice?

- How can the "third" discipline, referenced by Jon Iwata and Simon Sproule, be best exemplified in the organization? How is it defined, and how is it recruited for? What in-house or externally-sourced training is appropriate to grow the new breed of integrated marketer?

- How is the organization positioned to engage and participate in the interactive relationship with the global consumer and other important stakeholders? Which discipline owns or shares the digital and/or social media space? How can owned media be leveraged with other channels? And how can the organization create "total solutions" for its constituencies, which include online or mobile blended together with experiential and traditional media channels?

- Can PR be leveraged as a strategic marketing tool to help drive influence and advocacy for the brand, build reputational aspects, and provide the "glue" that leverages the organization's paid, owned, and earned media profile?

- What new audiences need to be addressed that could help to further the marketing and business goals, for example, employees, NGOs, retail partners, experts, and so on? And in what key geographic markets do they need to be engaged?

- Can "purpose" and social responsibility provide value to the brand and its reputation in multiple markets in order to drive brand preference and purchase?

- What new sources for analytics need to be identified and brought on board? How can new insights inform planning? What new metrics can help define success?

- What agency network partners are best-suited to address global or regional needs from a strategic perspective? How globally adept does an agency partner need to be? What skills are most important, for example, digital prowess?

On the latter point, *Bloomberg Businessweek*[5] recently reported that, "Everyone is waiting for the big four advertising giants to fade away, but it turns out that being a lumbering behemoth in a digital world has its advantages." The big agencies are retooling their organizations and their offers around new technologies and channels. According to John Seifert, chairman of WPP's Ogilvy and Mather North America, "The last 24 months have been unbelievably painful in our industry. The fact is, what you don't read about in the blogs, is that we let 391 people go. But we also hired 270 new people. We transferred another 300 people between different parts of the company. All of that was designed to meet the changing requirements of our business."[6]

There has been much talk and experimentation with smaller, more seemingly nimble, hot shops. But as David Lubars, chairman and chief creative officer of Omnicom's BBDO North America says in his interview with *Bloomberg Businessweek*, "All these little companies with fun names, we've kicked their butts." The big agencies are reconfiguring their workforces and their businesses to adapt to the new environment. Matt Donovan, Managing Partner of McCann Erickson, New York, says, "More and more companies are finding that the big agencies have retooled and do understand this change. We are paid by businesses to outsmart others. That's what we're here to do."[7]

Where does that leave the other types of agencies? Clearly the bigger agencies, whether they are in advertising or PR or market research, have the upper hand when it comes to both the geographic reach and the international mindset which are increasingly important aspects for marketers who need to navigate the global marketplace. Sharing best practice between countries or regions and encouraging mobility of their executives so that they can gain international experience will become increasingly important, as will having processes in place to coordinate international assignments and relationships.

---

5   *Bloomberg Businessweek*, "Don Draper's Revenge" by Felix Gillette, November 24, 2010.
6   *Bloomberg Businessweek*, "Don Draper's Revenge" by Felix Gillette, November 24, 2010.
7   *Bloomberg Businessweek*, "Don Draper's Revenge" by Felix Gillette, November 24, 2010.

Conclusion

"I've seen the power of PR grow as an industry, and at P&G," said Marc Pritchard, global marketing and brand building officer of P&G when he spoke at the Council of Public Relations Firms' (CPRF) Critical Issues Forum in 2010. "I'm a big fan of PR. In fact, I want to let you in on a secret: My Dad was in marketing and the first thing he taught me about marketing was about the power of PR...PR is the best form of marketing because it is the most authentic form of marketing...And from that point on, I made a commitment to fully leverage the power of PR in marketing."

Pritchard gives a host of reasons why "PR will continue to grow its impact in the future:

- PR is the great amplifier to make big ideas even bigger.

- PR starts and builds meaningful conversations and human interactions about a brand and its benefit.

- PR helps to shape deeper brand relationships.

- PR inherently invites participation because it involves word-of-mouth advocacy. I believe that PR and social media are inseparable – or at least close cousins – and that opens up new possibilities for engagement on a one-to-one and one-to-many basis.

- PR is authentic. It plays a central role in building a brand's credibility, and in today's transparent world, the advocates for a brand must truly believe in the brand and the company – whether that is a celebrity, influencer or a consumer."[1]

---

1   Council of PR Firms Critical Issues Forum presentation script, October 27, 2010.

Clearly the time has come for PR to shine with a key role in marketing and brand building. Never before has the convergence between marketing and PR been more acute, driven mainly by the immediacy of the Information Age, the proliferation of social platforms, and the resulting consumer democracy which, in turn, lends added weight to the importance of brand reputation.

From the interviews contained in this book and additional intelligence gleaned over the last 18 months, it's clear that the organizations that have succeeded most in blending the two disciplines have merged them under the marketing umbrella. In this way, there can be no confusion over the central leadership and vision, despite matrix structures existing in some circumstances to cater for regional BUs or vertical businesses. At the very least, some KPIs must be shared in order to engender collaboration.

Although the marketing pioneers featured here are from all walks of marketing – consumer brands and business brands, large and small – they do have five key things in common:

1. **Strong Leadership**: For the most part, their CEOs or leaders have been major sources of encouragement and, in some cases, have even led the reorganization within the marketing discipline. These leaders are interested in better globalizing their business, increasing efficiencies in marketing communication as a means to an end, and building a better platform from which to communicate and engage with, not to, their stakeholders.

2. **Boldness in Planning**: Experimentation is promoted and transparency across the marketing team is key. Planning processes are in place to encourage open dialogue around shared goals and resources to reduce traditional silo mentalities.

3. **Multi-Stakeholder Approach**: The aim of marketing is far broader than customers, be they consumer or business customers, to include employees and other key influencers and audiences who could advocate for a brand, or the company or organization.

4. **Shared KPIs**: Shared accountability is baked into each of these marketing teams. And CMOs have augmented traditional metrics with new forms of analytics, and they continue to increase the emphasis on data. In many cases, these CMOs are forging stronger relationships with their peers in Finance as well.

5. **Talent Aspirations**: Training, advancement, and mobility are stimulated within the marketing function to inspire new thinking and provide new opportunities. And recruitment needs are often revisited and readjusted based on the constantly changing environment and vision for the marketing discipline.

They also have in common the fact that they are not from traditional marketing backgrounds, but rather communications or varied other backgrounds. Does this give them an advantage on integrating their practices? Possibly yes. They all point to a heightened awareness of the importance of authenticity, transparency, engagement, participation, and "story-telling" – the ability to communicate clearly around a brand message or product proposition – the latter being increasingly important from a content perspective.

Because of their background, these CMOs also understand the importance of embracing the media. As Darryl Seibel of the BOA said, "We see how critical their role is in achieving larger organizational objectives. So a KPI for us would be how effective we are in creating that great line-meeting place where athletes, coaches, and media can get together and do the things they need to do. Recognizing that of course performance is priority one, we need to be able to tell these stories." Seibel can relate to past experiences where he's suffered pockets of media resistance. That just won't fly in this new age of transparency.

Their heritage of communications also leads them to take a multi-audience approach, more so than the traditional marketer. As Jon Iwata said, "The corporate PR job proceeds with an understanding that we have to think about all of the audiences and constituents that matter to us or that we matter to them. So you don't proceed with any sort of announcement without thinking about how the message is going to be understood or received by the media, management, retirees, community, suppliers, customers, and so on. It's second-nature to us. It is not second nature to the traditional marketer."

Are there disadvantages to not being a traditionally trained marketer? Probably yes again. The language of marketing is something that they've all had to learn, and analytics, which is increasing in importance to marketing, could be considered a weakness, and yet they all seem to have surrounded themselves with experts in this space who help navigate the way forward.

In many ways, these CMOs see their role as conduits for the greater good of marketing within their organizations. Amy Curtis-McIntyre called herself a "conductor" and Simon Sproule referred to himself as "air traffic control."

Clearly they need a vision for their brands and their businesses, but they also need to orchestrate and coordinate insights and intelligence, ideas, and best practice.

Where is the future of marketing? Iwata believes that the traditional model of marketing is breaking down. The marketing funnel is broken and the "4Ps" (the marketing mix combination of product, price, place – distribution, and promotion) don't operate as they have historically. He and Sproule talked of the need for a third type of marketing professional who will be much more comfortable with integration rather than thinking in the traditional marketing and PR silos. Beth Comstock advocated for commercial innovation in marketing, and Ann Lewnes stressed the importance of creativity.

Any advice for PR professionals wanting to take a more active role in integrated marketing? Pritchard had some words of wisdom as closing thoughts to his CPRF presentation:

- "Get experience in all forms of marketing and brand building. Brand building is a team sport, and you don't need to play all positions, but you need to know enough to make sure the team operates as an integrated and powerful force.

- Stake your claim in digital. Make digital and social media absolutely integral in how you operate. It is a critical communications capability to listen, engage, and create conversations with people and get them to participate in our brand communities.

- Create big ideas. PR can both start conversations and amplify ideas, so your role is critical in driving big ideas that build brands and invite participation."

Index

103

Making the Connections:
Using Internal Communication to Turn Strategy into Action
Bill Quirke
Paperback: 978-0-566-08780-6
ebook: 978-1-4094-0516-0

The CEO: Chief Engagement Officer:
Turning Hierarchy Upside Down to Drive Performance
John Smythe
Paperback: 978-0-566-08561-1
ebook: 978-0-7546-8180-9

The Psychology of Marketing:
Cross-Cultural Perspectives
Gerhard Raab, G. Jason Goddard,
Riad A. Ajami and Alexander Unger
Hardback: 978-0-566-08903-9
ebook: 978-0-566-08904-6

Visit **www.gowerpublishing.com** and

- search the entire catalogue of Gower books in print
- order titles online at 10% discount
- take advantage of special offers
- sign up for our monthly e-mail update service
- download free sample chapters from all recent titles
- download or order our catalogue